REVISED
AND
UPDATED

SPIRITUAL
DISCIPLINES
FOR THE
CHRISTIAN
LIFE

DONALD S. WHITNEY

STUDY GUIDE

NAVPRESS

A NavPress published resource in alliance
with Tyndale House Publishers, Inc.

NAVPRESS⬤®

NavPress is the publishing ministry of The Navigators, an international Christian organization and leader in personal spiritual development. NavPress is committed to helping people grow spiritually and enjoy lives of meaning and hope through personal and group resources that are biblically rooted, culturally relevant, and highly practical.

For more information, go to www.NavPress.com.

© 1994, 2014 by Donald S. Whitney

A NavPress published resource in alliance with Tyndale House Publishers, Inc.

All rights reserved. No part of this publication may be reproduced in any form without written permission from NavPress, P.O. Box 35001, Colorado Springs, CO 80935. www.navpress.com

NAVPRESS and the NAVPRESS logo are registered trademarks of NavPress. Absence of ® in connection with marks of NavPress or other parties does not indicate an absence of registration of those marks.

TYNDALE is a registered trademark of Tyndale House Publishers, Inc.

ISBN 978-1-61521-618-5

Cover photograph of book copyright © Ariusz Nawrocki/Shutterstock. All rights reserved.

Cover photograph of paper copyright © Ragnarock/Shutterstock. All rights reserved.

Cover photograph of fabric copyright © frescomovie/Shutterstock. All rights reserved.

Some of the anecdotal illustrations in this book are true to life and are included with the permission of the persons involved. All other illustrations are composites of real situations, and any resemblance to people living or dead is coincidental.

Unless otherwise indicated, all Scripture quotations are taken from *The Holy Bible*, English Standard Version® (ESV®), copyright © 2001 by Crossway, a publishing ministry of Good News Publishers. Used by permission. All rights reserved. Scripture quotations marked NIV are taken from the Holy Bible, *New International Version,*® NIV.® Copyright © 1973, 1978, 1984, 2011 by Biblica, Inc.® Used by permission of Zondervan. All rights reserved worldwide. www.zondervan.com. Scripture quotations marked NASB are taken from the New American Standard Bible,® copyright © 1960, 1962, 1963, 1968, 1971, 1972, 1973, 1975, 1977, 1995 by The Lockman Foundation. Used by permission.

Printed in the United States of America

19	18	17	16	
6	5	4	3	2

Contents

THE SPIRITUAL DISCIPLINES . . . FOR THE PURPOSE OF GODLINESS

Discipline yourself for the purpose of godliness.
(1 TIMOTHY 4:7, NASB)

CENTRAL IDEA

The only road to Christian maturity passes through the practice of the Spiritual Disciplines. These personal and interpersonal activities given by God in the Bible have been practiced by God's people since biblical times. They are the sufficient means Christians are to use in the Spirit-filled pursuit of godliness, that is, closeness to Christ and conformity to Christ. Jesus modeled them for us and expects us to pursue them. In doing so, we will taste the joy of a spiritually disciplined lifestyle.

WARM-UP

1. Describe a time when you disciplined yourself in order to reach a specific goal or when you did not discipline yourself and failed to reach a specific goal.

    _____

    _____

    _____

What Is the Purpose of Spiritual Disciplines?

When it comes to discipline in the Christian life, many believers feel it's discipline without direction. Prayer threatens to be drudgery. The practical value of meditation on Scripture seems uncertain. The real purpose of a discipline like fasting is often unclear.

The Bible says of God's elect, "For those whom he foreknew he also predestined to be conformed to the image of his Son" (Romans 8:29). God's eternal plan ensures that every Christian will ultimately conform to Christlikeness. We will be changed "when he appears" so that "we shall be like him" (1 John 3:2). This is no vision; this is you, Christian, as soon as "he appears."

So why all the talk about discipline? If God has predestined our conformity to Christlikeness, where does discipline fit in? Although God will grant Christlikeness to us when Jesus returns, until then He intends for us to grow toward it. We aren't merely to wait for holiness; we're to pursue it. "Strive for peace with everyone," we're commanded in Hebrews 12:14, "and for the holiness without which no one will see the Lord."

This leads us to ask what every Christian should ask: "How then shall I pursue holiness? How can I be like Jesus Christ, the Son of God?" We find a clear answer in 1 Timothy 4:7: "Discipline yourself for the purpose of godliness" (NASB).

The only road to Christian maturity and godliness (a biblical term synonymous with Christlikeness and holiness) passes through the practice of the Spiritual Disciplines. Godliness is the goal of the Disciplines, and when we remember this, the Spiritual Disciplines can become a delight instead of drudgery.

God Commands Us to Be Holy

The original language of the words "discipline yourself for the purpose of godliness" makes it plain that this is a command of God, not merely a suggestion. Holiness is not an option for those who claim to be children of the Holy One (see 1 Peter 1:15-16), so neither are the means of holiness—that is, the Spiritual Disciplines—an option.

The expectation of disciplined spirituality is implied in Jesus' offer of Matthew 11:29: "Take my yoke upon you, and learn from me." The same is true in this offer of discipleship: "And he said to all, 'If anyone would come after me, let him deny himself and take up his cross daily and follow me'" (Luke 9:23). These verses tell us that to be a disciple of Jesus means, at the very least, to learn from and follow Him. Learning and following involve discipline, for those who learn only incidentally and follow accidentally are not true disciples. That discipline is at the heart of discipleship is confirmed by Galatians 5:22-23, which says that spiritual self-discipline (implied in "self-control") is one of the most evident marks of being Spirit-controlled.

The Lord Jesus not only expects these biblical Spiritual Disciplines of those who follow Him, He is the model of discipline for the purpose of godliness.

What Are the Spiritual Disciplines?

First, the Bible prescribes *both personal and interpersonal* Spiritual Disciplines. Some Spiritual Disciplines—like private prayer—we practice alone; others—like small group or congregational prayer—we practice with other Christians. Second, Spiritual Disciplines are *activities, not attitudes*. Disciplines are practices, not character qualities, graces, or "fruit of the Spirit" (Galatians 5:22-23). Third, the subject matter of this book is limited to those Spiritual Disciplines that are *biblical*, that is, to practices taught or modeled in the Bible. Fourth, this book takes the position that the Spiritual Disciplines found in Scripture are *sufficient* for knowing and experiencing God, and for growing in Christlikeness. Fifth, the Spiritual Disciplines are practices *derived from the gospel, not divorced from the gospel*. When the Disciplines are rightly practiced, they take us deeper into the gospel of Jesus and its glories, not away from it as though we've moved on to more advanced levels of Christianity. Sixth, the Spiritual Disciplines are *means* to godliness, *not ends* to be practiced for their own sake.

So the Spiritual Disciplines[1] are those personal and interpersonal activities given by God in the Bible as the sufficient means believers in Jesus Christ are to use in the Spirit-filled, gospel-driven pursuit of godliness, that is, closeness to Christ and conformity to Christ. They are the habits of devotion and experiential Christianity that have been practiced by the people of God since biblical times.

Whatever the Discipline, its most important feature is its *purpose*. Just as there is little value in practicing the scales on a guitar or piano apart from the purpose of playing music, so there is little value in practicing Spiritual Disciplines apart from the single purpose that unites them (see Colossians 2:20-23; 1 Timothy 4:8). That purpose is godliness. Thus we are told in 1 Timothy 4:7 to discipline ourselves "for the purpose of *godliness*" (emphasis added).

On the one hand, we recognize that even the most iron-willed self-discipline by itself will not make us more holy, for growth in holiness is a gift from God (see John 7:17; 1 Thessalonians 5:23; Hebrews 2:11). On the other hand, that doesn't mean that we're to do nothing to pursue godliness, just living the life we want until and unless God decides to make us holy. What we are to do is discipline ourselves "for the purpose of godliness," practicing the God-given Spiritual Disciplines as a means of receiving His grace and growing in Christlikeness.

Think of the Spiritual Disciplines as ways by which we can spiritually place ourselves in the path of God's grace and seek Him (see Luke 19:1-10), much like Zacchaeus placed himself physically in Jesus' path and sought Him. The Lord, by His Spirit, still travels down certain paths, paths that He Himself has ordained and revealed in Scripture. We call these paths the Spiritual Disciplines, and if we will place ourselves on these paths and look for Him there by faith, we can expect to encounter Him. By means of these Bible-based practices, we consciously place ourselves before God in anticipation of enjoying His presence and receiving His transforming grace.

The Fruit of Spiritual Disciplines

We must remember that the mature freedoms of discipline-nurtured godliness do not develop in a single reading through the Bible or in a few forays through some of the other Disciplines. Scripture reminds us that self-control, such as that expressed through the Spiritual Disciplines, must persevere before it ripens into the mature fruit of godliness. Observe closely the sequence of development in 2 Peter 1:6: "and to self-control, perseverance; and to perseverance, godliness" (NIV). Godliness is a lifelong pursuit.

If your picture of a disciplined Christian is one of a grim, tight-lipped, joyless half-robot, then you've missed the point. Jesus was the most disciplined Man who ever lived and yet the most joyful and truly alive. As our Lord and our Redeemer and more, Jesus is not merely our example, still He is our example of discipline. Let us follow Him to joy through the Spiritual Disciplines. (Taken from chapter 1 of *Spiritual Disciplines for the Christian Life.*)

Persevering in the Practice of the Spiritual Disciplines

There are three matters that are indispensible in helping you persevere in the practice of the Spiritual Disciplines: the role of the Holy Spirit, the role of fellowship, and the role of struggle in Christian living.

The Holy Spirit. The role of the Holy Spirit is to produce within us the desire and the power for the Disciplines that lead to godliness. That He develops this in every believer is evident from 2 Timothy 1:7.

The Bible doesn't explain the mechanics of the mystery of the Spirit's ministry to us. But these two things are clear: (1) the Holy Spirit will be ever faithful to help each of God's elect to persevere to the end in those things that will make us like Christ, and (2) we must not harden our hearts, but instead respond to His promptings if we would be godly.

Fellowship. No one should read of the Spiritual Disciplines and imagine that by practicing them in isolation from other believers he or she can be as Christlike—perhaps even more so—than Christians who are active members of a local body of Christ. Anyone who measures progress in Christlikeness only in terms of growth in his or her fellowship with God takes an incomplete measurement, for spiritual maturity also includes growth in fellowship with the children of God. The apostle John juxtaposed these two in 1 John 1:3. As New Testament fellowship is with both the triune God and His people, so spiritual growth incorporates both a vertical and a horizontal dimension. Moreover, biblical fellowship will encourage your persevering practice of the personal Spiritual Disciplines.

Struggle. Although "trust" and "rest" are core values of the Christian life, so are "discipline" and "struggle." Many forces combat the spiritual progress of those still on this side of heaven. Because of the world, the flesh, and the Devil, practicing the Spiritual Disciplines and progressing in godliness will be accompanied by struggle (compare Colossians 1:29; 1 Timothy 4:10). The victory that we actually experience in daily life over the forces opposing our progress in the Disciplines comes *through the practice of the Disciplines.* (Taken from chapter 13 of *Spiritual Disciplines for the Christian Life.*)

Pondering Spiritual Disciplines

2. In the past, how have you felt about Spiritual Disciplines such as Bible intake, prayer, worship, evangelism, and fasting? Be honest.

_____

_____

_____

3. What single purpose unites the Spiritual Disciplines? (See 1 Timothy 4:7.)

_____

_____

_____

The Importance of Holiness (Godliness)

4. What does 1 Peter 1:15-16 say about the importance of holiness in believers' lives?

_____

_____

_____

5. Describe a godly person you know who has reached spiritual maturity through discipline. Which practical Spiritual Disciplines has he or she practiced regularly?

_____

_____

_____

Catalysts That God Uses to Make Us More Christlike

6. *People.* Often God brings people into our lives whose input leads us to become more Christlike. Read Proverbs 27:17. Describe a time when God used someone to file away your rough, ungodly edges.

_____

_____

_____

7. a. *Circumstances.* We've all faced trying circumstances that God uses to make us more like Himself. What does Romans 8:28 say about our difficult circumstances?

_____

_____

_____

b. As a group, discuss how God uses circumstances in life to move you closer toward godliness.

_____

8. *Spiritual Disciplines.* Rather than externally coming from people and/or circumstances, this catalyst works from the inside of our lives and goes outward. Also, God grants us more choice regarding our involvement with this catalyst than with people or circumstances. Describe a time when God used your prayer time or Bible meditation to change you from the inside out.

_____

_____

_____

_____

Spiritual Disciplines: A Way to Seek God and Know Him Better

Today people place great emphasis on physical exercise as a means of staying healthy. Spiritual Disciplines are similar to physical exercise, in that when we exercise ourselves spiritually we promote spiritual health and growth—godliness—in our lives.

Let's look at two Bible stories that reveal how two people put themselves in the path of Jesus and sought Him. As a result, their lives were forever changed.

9. Bartimaeus: Luke 18:35-43
   a. What strikes you about his response to Jesus?

_____

_____

_____

b. In response to Bartimaeus's faith, what did Jesus do for him?

_____

_____

_____

_____

10. Zacchaeus: Luke 19:1-10
    a. How did this tax collector pursue Jesus?

_____

_____

_____

_____

    b. What does this story tell us about Jesus' mercy?

_____

_____

_____

_____

11. How do these stories encourage you to seek God?

_____

_____

_____

_____

The Spiritual Disciplines Are Like Placing Ourselves in God's Path

12. According to the text on page 13 of *Spiritual Disciplines for the Christian Life*, "by means of these Bible-based practices, we consciously place ourselves before God in anticipation of enjoying His presence and receiving His transforming grace." Describe a time when you placed yourself in God's path and His grace transformed you.

_____

_____

The Lord Expects Us to Pursue the Spiritual Disciplines

13. What do the following verses say about what it means for each of us to be Jesus' disciple?

Matthew 11:29 _____

_____

Luke 9:23 _____

_____

Galatians 5:22-23 _____

_____

The Consequences of Being Spiritually Undisciplined

14. Why do people who will discipline themselves for years to become proficient at their careers or recreational sports quickly stop pursuing the Spiritual Disciplines? Has this happened to you?

_____

_____

15. The text in chapter 1 of *Spiritual Disciplines for the Christian Life* describes people who are faithful to the church and demonstrate genuine enthusiasm for the things of God, yet spiritually they "are a mile wide and an inch deep." What are some positive and negative characteristics of these people? How does someone become like this? What does it mean that "they have dabbled in everything but disciplined themselves in nothing"? What would you need to do to ensure this never describes you?

_____

_____

_____

Spiritual Disciplines Bring Freedom

16. a. Freedom "comes through mastery of any discipline. . . . The freedom of godliness is the freedom to do what God calls us through Scripture to do and the freedom to express the character qualities of Christ through our own personality" (pages 17–18 in *Spiritual Disciplines for the Christian Life*). In which areas of life have you experienced this freedom?

_____

_____

_____

b. If you haven't experienced this freedom, what steps will you take to bring yourself closer to this freedom?

_____

_____

_____

Spiritual Disciplines Take Time

17. Read 2 Peter 1:3-6. Why must self-control persevere before the mature fruit of godliness ripens?

_____

_____

_____

_____

God Invites All Christians to Enjoy the Spiritual Disciplines

18. When we practice the Spiritual Disciplines with the goal of godliness in mind, our discipline has direction. Jesus, our Savior and our King, is also our example of discipline. Look up these verses: Matthew 4:2; Luke 2:46-47; John 13:2-6; 17:4. What does each say about Jesus and His pursuit of the Spiritual Disciplines?

_____

_____

_____

_____

Persevering in the Practice of the Spiritual Disciplines

19. Through the Holy Spirit, we have the power to persevere in the Spiritual Disciplines. Read 2 Timothy 1:7 and then describe why this truth should encourage us.

_____

_____

_____

_____

CLOSING PRAYER

Focus on God's deep love for you and on His desire to bless you through the Spiritual Disciplines. Ask the Lord to help you become willing to practice these Disciplines during the coming weeks of this study.

GOING DEEPER

(Extra questions for further study)

20. These days "denying oneself" is not a popular viewpoint. How does what Jesus said in Luke 9:23 relate to the practice of the Spiritual Disciplines?

21. Why is self-control one of the most evident marks of being Spirit-controlled? (See Galatians 5:22-23.)

22. What do you think the text of *Spiritual Disciplines for the Christian Life* on page 12 means by, "the Spiritual Disciplines [are] ways by which we can spiritually place ourselves in the path of God's grace and seek Him"?

23. According to 1 Corinthians 12:4-7, every believer in
     Christ has been given spiritual gifts. Why do you think
     Spiritual Discipline is so important in the development
     of these gifts?

     _____

     _____

     _____

     _____

24. What practical steps are you willing to take this coming
     week to begin building more Spiritual Discipline into
     your life?

     _____

     _____

     _____

     _____

BIBLE INTAKE (PART 1) . . . FOR THE PURPOSE OF GODLINESS

CENTRAL IDEA

No other Spiritual Discipline rivals the importance of the intake of God's Word. No other Spiritual Discipline can compensate for the lack of it. Without feasting on the food of Scripture, no one will enjoy a growing, healthy Christlike life. Bible intake is not only the most important Spiritual Discipline, it is also the most broad. It actually consists of several subdisciplines. It's much like a university comprised of many colleges, each specializing in a different discipline, yet all united under the general name of the university. The first three "colleges" of Bible intake are hearing, reading, and studying God's Word.

WARM-UP

1. Describe the Bible intake that took place—or didn't take place—in your home and church as you were growing

up. Has that affected your view of Bible intake today?
If so, how?

_____

_____

_____

_____

2. Have you—and your family, if you are married—
developed a consistent pattern of Bible intake? If so,
describe the difference it has made in your life. If not,
what keeps you from developing such a pattern?

_____

_____

_____

_____

The Importance of Bible Intake

No Spiritual Discipline is more important than the intake of God's
Word. Nothing can substitute for it. There simply is no healthy
Christian life apart from a diet of the milk and meat of Scripture.
The reasons for this are obvious.

In the Bible God tells us about Himself, and especially about
Jesus Christ, the Incarnation of God.

The Bible unfolds the Law of God to us and shows us how we've
all broken it. There we learn how Christ died as a sinless, willing
Substitute for breakers of God's Law and how we must repent and
believe in Him to be right with God.

In the Bible we learn the ways and will of the Lord. We find in
Scripture how God wants us to live, and what brings the most joy
and satisfaction in life.

None of this eternally essential information can be found any-where else except in the Bible. Therefore if we would know God and be godly, we must know the Word of God—intimately.

My pastoral experience bears witness to the validity of surveys that frequently reveal that great numbers of professing Christians know little more about the Bible than poor Christians in remote parts of the world who possess not even a shred of Scripture. So even though we honor God's Word with our lips, we must confess that our hearts—as well as our hands, ears, eyes, and minds—are often far from it. Regardless of how busy we become with all things Christian, we must remember that the most transforming practice available to us is the disciplined intake of Scripture.

Hearing God's Word

The easiest of the Disciplines related to the intake of God's Word is simply hearing it. Why consider this a Discipline? Because if we don't discipline ourselves to hear God's Word regularly, we may only hear it accidentally, just when we feel like it, or never hear it at all. For most of us, disciplining ourselves to hear God's Word means primarily developing the practice of attending a Bible-believing church where the Word of God is faithfully preached.

Jesus once said, "Blessed rather are those who hear the word of God and keep it!" (Luke 11:28). Merely listening to God-inspired words is not the point. The purpose of all methods of Bible intake is to "keep it," that is, to do what God says and thereby develop in Christlikeness.

One of the English Puritans, Jeremiah Burroughs, wrote before his death in 1646 the following words of counsel regarding prepa-ration for the discipline of hearing God's Word: "First, when you come to hear the Word, if you would sanctify God's name, you must possess your souls with what it is you are going to hear, that what you are going to hear is the Word of God."[1] So hearing the Word of God is not merely passive listening; it is a Discipline to be cultivated.

Reading God's Word

USA Today reported a poll that showed only 11 percent of all Americans—Christian and non-Christian—read the Bible every day. More than half read it less than once a month or never at all.[2] A survey taken less than a year earlier by the Barna Research Group among those claiming to be "born-again Christians" disclosed these disheartening numbers: Only 18 percent—less than two of every ten—read the Bible every day. Worst of all, 23 percent—almost one in four professing Christians—say they *never* read the Word of God.[3]

Because "all Scripture is breathed out by God and profitable for teaching, for reproof, for correction, and for training in righteousness" (2 Timothy 3:16), shouldn't we read it?

Jesus often asked questions about people's understanding of the Scriptures, sometimes beginning with the words, "Have you not read . . . ?" (Matthew 19:4; Mark 12:10). He assumed that those claiming to be the people of God would have read the Word of God. When He said, "Man shall not live by bread alone, but by every word that comes from the mouth of God" (Matthew 4:4), surely He intended at the very least for us to read "every word."

Here are the three most practical suggestions for consistent success in Bible reading.

First, find the time. Discipline yourself to find the time. Try to make it the same time every day.

Second, find a Bible-reading plan. It's no wonder that those who simply open the Bible at random each day soon drop the discipline. Bible-reading plans abound on the Internet. Many study Bibles contain a reading schedule somewhere within the pages. Most local churches can provide you with a daily reading guide also.

Third, find at least one word, phrase, or verse to meditate on each time you read. (We'll look at meditation more closely in the next lesson.) Take at least one thing you've read and think deeply about it for a few moments. Your insight into Scripture will deepen and you'll better understand how it applies to your life.

Studying God's Word

If reading the Bible can be compared to cruising the width of a clear, sparkling lake in a motorboat, studying the Bible is like slowly crossing that same lake in a glass-bottomed boat. The motorboat crossing provides an overview of the lake and a swift, passing view of its depths. The glass-bottomed boat of study, however, takes you beneath the surface of Scripture for an unhurried look of clarity and detail that's normally missed by those who simply read the text.

Why do so many Christians neglect the study of God's Word? R. C. Sproul said it painfully well:

> Here then, is the real problem of our negligence. We fail in our duty to study God's Word not so much because it is difficult to understand, not so much because it is dull and boring, but because it is work. Our problem is not a lack of intelligence or a lack of passion. Our problem is that we are lazy.[4]

The basic difference between Bible reading and Bible study is simply a pen and paper (or some other means of preserving your thoughts). Books, thick and thin, abound on how to study the Bible.

So discipline yourself for the purpose of godliness by committing to at least one way of improving your intake of the Holy Word of God—by hearing, by reading, or by studying. For those who use their Bibles little are really not much better off than those who have no Bibles at all. (Taken from chapter 2 of *Spiritual Disciplines for the Christian Life.*)

The Importance of Bible Intake

3. Do you agree that "there simply is no healthy Christian life apart from a diet of the milk and meat of Scripture"? Why or why not?

---

4. How might your beliefs be different if you did not have a Bible? If you never received Bible intake?

_____

_____

_____

5. Why is knowing the Bible intimately such a vital part of knowing God and being godly?

_____

_____

_____

6. The text states that we often honor God's Word only with our lips. In what practical ways might you add to that honor with your heart, hands, ears, eyes, and mind?

_____

_____

_____

_____

7. In our busy lives, it's easy to become preoccupied with "Christian" activities and not spend enough time in God's Word. What "Christian" activities are you involved in? In what ways is or is not Bible intake a part of these activities?

_____

_____

_____

Hearing God's Word

8. Read Luke 11:28. Why do you think Jesus emphasizes this point?

9. If we aren't disciplined in hearing God's Word, which negative consequences will occur? Be specific.

10. What do the following verses say about hearing God's Word?

    Romans 10:17 _____

    1 Timothy 4:13 _____

11. What other ways, besides in a local church ministry, can you hear God's Word?

12. Why is it important not to be a passive listener to God's Word? How can you cultivate the ability to be an intent listener? Be specific.

_____

_____

_____

Reading God's Word

13. Read 1 Timothy 4:7 and 2 Timothy 3:16. How much time, on the average, do you spend reading the Bible each day? Be honest.

_____

_____

_____

_____

14. What happens to a person who reads the Bible? (See Revelation 1:3.)

_____

_____

_____

15. In the past, have you seen a connection between the time you spend in Bible intake and your knowledge of God and His power? Describe your experiences.

_____

_____

_____

16. Why can Bible intake become a chore instead of a
     Discipline of joy? In what ways might meditating on
     Scripture deepen your appreciation of God's Word?

_____

_____

_____

_____

Studying God's Word

17. a. Consider Ezra 7:10. To which three key areas of study
         did Ezra devote himself?

_____

_____

_____

     b. What did he do before he began teaching God's Word
         to the people?

_____

_____

_____

18. In 2 Timothy 4:13, Paul asked Timothy to bring several
     items. What does Paul's request communicate to us about
     the importance of studying God's Word?

_____

_____

_____

19. Do you agree with R. C. Sproul that laziness is the real reason Christians don't study God's Word enough? Why or why not?

_____

_____

_____

20. What, in your mind, are the differences between hearing, reading, and studying God's Word?

_____

_____

_____

CLOSING PRAYER

Focus on thanking God for sharing His Word with you. Ask Him to help you develop the Discipline of regular Bible intake so you can get to know Him better. Express your need for Him and His truths in your daily life.

GOING DEEPER

(Extra questions for further study)

21. If your growth in godliness were measured by the quality of your Bible intake, how would you measure up?

_____

_____

22. What do you think Jesus meant when He prayed, "Sanctify them in the truth; your word is truth" (John 17:17)?

23. How does the emphasis of Philippians 3:13 apply to the failure many of us have experienced in daily Bible intake?

24. What can you do today to improve your intake of God's Word in the areas of hearing, reading, and studying?

25. Why is it important to continually receive Bible intake if such intake doesn't emotionally uplift you or give you a sense of peace each time?

26. How do you think you'll feel when you finally see the Word of God in the flesh, in heaven? How can this

perspective encourage you in your commitment to know God more deeply today?

_____

_____

_____

27. Consider how the following might enhance your study of Scripture:

- Writing down observations and questions about what you read
- Looking up cross-references
- Finding key words and seeing how they're used in other Scripture portions
- Outlining chapters, one paragraph at a time
- Doing book studies, character studies, topical studies, and/or word studies

BIBLE INTAKE (PART 2) . . . FOR THE PURPOSE OF GODLINESS

CENTRAL IDEA

The intake of God's Word is the most important Spiritual Discipline. We practice this Discipline not only by hearing, reading, and studying God's Word, but also through memorizing and meditating on Scripture, and by applying what we learn to our daily lives. When rightly practiced, these promote increased knowledge of God and closer conformity to Christ.

WARM-UP

1. How much time have you begun setting aside each day to hear, read, and/or study the Bible, as we talked about in the last lesson? What are you gaining from this time? Is this the right amount of time for you?

   _____

   _____

   _____

2. Which verses that you have memorized have special meaning to you?

_____

_____

_____

_____

Memorizing God's Word

Many Christians look on the Spiritual Discipline of memorizing God's Word as something tantamount to modern-day martyrdom. Why? Perhaps because many associate all memorization with the memory efforts required of them in school. It was work, and most of it was uninteresting and of limited value. Frequently heard, also, is the excuse of having a bad memory. But what if I offered you one thousand dollars for every verse you could memorize in the next seven days? Do you think your attitude toward Scripture memory and your ability to memorize would improve? Any financial reward would be minimal when compared to the accumulating value of the treasure of God's Word deposited within your mind.

Memorization Strengthens Your Faith and Ministry

What Christian doesn't want his or her faith strengthened? One thing you can do to strengthen it is to discipline yourself to memorize Scripture. Memorizing Scripture strengthens your faith because it repeatedly reinforces the truth, often just when you need to hear it again.

On the Day of Pentecost (the Jewish holiday being celebrated when the Holy Spirit came in great power upon Jesus' followers), the apostle Peter was suddenly inspired by God to stand and preach to the crowd about Jesus. Much of what he said consisted of quotations from the Old Testament (see Acts 2:14-40).

Although there's a qualitative difference between Peter's uniquely inspired sermon and our Spirit-led conversations, his experience illustrates how Scripture memory can prepare us for unexpected witnessing or counseling opportunities. But until the verses are hidden in the heart, they aren't available to use with the mouth.

Memorization Supplies Spiritual Guidance and Power

The psalmist wrote, "Your testimonies are my delight; they are my counselors" (Psalm 119:24). Just as the Holy Spirit retrieves scriptural truth from our memory banks for use in counseling others, so also will He bring it to our own minds in providing timely guidance for ourselves.

When Scripture is stored in the mind, it is available for the Holy Spirit to bring to your attention when you need it most. That's why the author of Psalm 119 wrote, "I have stored up your word in my heart, that I might not sin against you" (verse 11). It's one thing, for instance, to be watching or thinking about something when you know you shouldn't, but there's added power against the temptation when a specific verse can be brought to your mind, like Colossians 3:2: "Set your minds on things that are above, not on things that are on earth."

Memorization Stimulates Meditation

One of the most underrated benefits of memorizing Scripture is that it provides fuel for meditation. When you have memorized a verse of Scripture, you can meditate on it anywhere at any time during the day or night. There are many good prepackaged Scripture memory resources available in print and digital formats. But you might prefer selecting verses yourself on a particular topic where the Lord is working in your life right now. If your faith is weak, for example, memorize verses on faith. If you're struggling with a habit, find verses that will help you experience victory over it.

Tips on Scripture Memory

A. Make a list of the verses on-screen or on a sheet of paper or index cards.
B. Draw picture reminders to trigger your memory of key words in the verses.
C. Memorize the verses perfectly, word for word, with each reference.
D. Find someone who will hold you accountable for your memory work and will review verses with you.
E. Every day, review some of the verses you have previously memorized and meditate on them.

Meditating on God's Word—Benefits and Methods

One sad feature of our contemporary culture is that meditation has become identified more with non-Christian systems of thought than with biblical Christianity. But we must remember that meditation is both commanded by God and modeled by the godly in Scripture. So let's define *meditation* as deep thinking on the truths and spiritual realities revealed in Scripture, or upon life from a scriptural perspective, for the purposes of understanding, application, and prayer.

The kind of meditation encouraged in the Bible differs from other kinds of meditation in several ways. For instance, while some advocate a kind of meditation in which you do your best to empty your mind, Christian meditation involves filling your mind with God and the truth of God. For some, meditation is an attempt to achieve complete mental passivity, but biblical meditation requires constructive mental activity. Worldly meditation employs visualization techniques intended to "create your own reality," and while Christian history has always had a place for the sanctified use of our God-given imagination in meditation, imagination is our servant to help us meditate on things that are true (see Philippians 4:8). Furthermore, instead of "creating our own reality" through visualization, we link meditation with prayer to God and responsible, Spirit-filled human action to effect changes.

How Then Do We Meditate Christianly?

After your Bible reading, choose the verse, phrase, or word that impresses you most from the passage of Scripture you've read. If nothing attracted particular attention, choose one of the most important verses from the section you read. Then use one of the following methods to meditate on the text.

The general rule in your personal, daily intake of Scripture is to both read and meditate. Read at length—such as a chapter or more—then go back over what you've read and select something specific from that as the focus of your meditation. Read big; meditate small.

- Review the verse repeatedly, emphasizing a different word each time. So with Jesus' declaration, "I am the resurrection and the life" (John 11:25), you would consider the verse at least seven times, emphasizing a different word each of the seven times.
- Rewrite the verse or phrase in your own words.
- Formulate a principle from the text, asking what this particular text teaches.
- Think of an illustration of the text. What story, object, event, or similar item pictures or explains it?
- Look for applications of the text. What should you do in response to it? After your meditation, you should be able to name one (or more) definite response(s) or action(s) you will make because of what you have read.
- Ask how the text points to some aspect of God's Law or to the gospel.
- Ask how the text points to something about the person and work of Jesus.

- Ask what question is answered or what problem is solved by the text.
- Pray through the text. Turn the words of the text into prayer. Talk to God about the things that come to mind as you consider the verse or passage.
- Memorize the text.
- Create an artistic expression of the text. Compose a song, poem, or sketch based on the text.
- Ask the Philippians 4:8 questions of the text. (See pages 63–65 in *Spiritual Disciplines for the Christian Life* for a further explanation of this method and the Joseph Hall questions below.)
- Ask the Joseph Hall questions of the text.
- Set, then discover a minimum number of insights into the text.
- Find a link or common thread between all the paragraphs or chapters you read.
- Ask how the text speaks to your current issue or question.
- Use "meditation mapping." (See pages 67–68 in *Spiritual Disciplines for the Christian Life* or see online or printed resources on "mind mapping," and apply those principles of note taking to recording your meditations on Scripture.)

Don't rush through the biblical text. Read less—if necessary—in order to have adequate time for meditation. So if you have only ten minutes, don't read for ten minutes. Read for five minutes, then meditate for five minutes. Far better to read less and remember something, than to read more and remember nothing.

The Value of Applying God's Word

The Bible promises the blessing of God on those who apply the Word of God to their lives. The classic New Covenant statement on the value of integrating the spiritual with the concrete is James 1:22-25. Pithy and powerful is Jesus' similar statement, "If you know these things, blessed are you if you do them" (John 13:17).

Despite the difficulty and spiritual opposition, are you willing, at all costs, to begin using your mind "in a disciplined way"[1] to feed on the Word of God "for the purpose of godliness"? (Taken from chapter 3 of *Spiritual Disciplines for the Christian Life.*)

Exploring Scripture Memorization

3. How does Jesus' confrontation with Satan (see Matthew 4:1-11) illustrate the power of Scripture that is committed to memory?

---

4. Read Proverbs 22:17-19. Why should we keep God's Word within us and ready on our lips?

---

5. Describe a time, if you can, when Scripture memory helped you during a witnessing or counseling opportunity. Share your experience with the group.

---

6. What does Psalm 119:24 say about guidance? How might you apply this truth to your busy life?

7. What was the psalmist's attitude toward Scripture? (See all of Psalm 119, but especially verse 97.)

Exploring Biblical Meditation

8. Name several differences between biblical meditation and other kinds of meditation.

9. Read Joshua 1:8. What did God command Joshua to do, and what did God promise would happen as a result of Joshua's obedience?

10. What do you think it means to meditate on God's Word throughout the day and night?

11. Which aspects of daily life distract you from concentrating your thoughts on God and His wisdom, and what will you do to overcome these distractions?

12. As we meditate on Scripture, what happens to our minds? (See Romans 12:2.)

Applying God's Word to Our Daily Lives

13. Read James 1:22-25. When you read the Bible, do you find it easy to apply what you read to your life? Why or why not?

14. a. Sometimes Christians use verses incorrectly to try to prove a certain point. Why is it so important for people to understand the meaning of particular verses in context before applying the verses to their lives?

b. Why is an overall Bible intake through hearing, reading, studying, memorizing, and meditating on Scripture so important?

15. Consider this statement: "Biblical meditation isn't an end in itself; it is the key to putting the truths and realities of Scripture into practice." Do you agree? Why or why not?

16. What steps will you take to deal with the obstacles you expect to face as you begin to memorize God's Word?

17. What three steps can you take this week to cultivate the Discipline of meditating on God's Word?

CLOSING PRAYER

Ask God to open your eyes and show you the wonderful truths in His Word. Praise Him for who He is and ask Him to guide you as you seek to apply biblical truths in your life this coming week.

GOING DEEPER

(Extra questions for further study)

18. List several of your concerns and personal needs. Find verses that apply to each concern and need, and memorize them before next week's meeting.

19. The Bible refers to three general objects of meditation: (1) God's Word, (2) God's works, and (3) God's attributes.

Using the following chart, write down specific objects of meditation found in each of these verses:

God's Word:	Joshua 1:8	
	Psalm 1:2	
	Psalm 119:15 (two objects here)	
	Psalm 119:23	
	Psalm 119:48	
	Psalm 119:78	
	Psalm 119:97	
	Psalm 119:99	
	Psalm 119:148	
God's Works:	Psalm 77:12 (two objects here)	
	Psalm 119:27	
	Psalm 143:5 (two objects here)	
	Psalm 145:5	
God's Attributes:	Psalm 63:6	
	Psalm 145:5	

PRAYER . . .
FOR THE PURPOSE OF GODLINESS

CENTRAL IDEA

Prayer is a vital Spiritual Discipline, second only to the intake of God's Word. To be like Jesus, we must pray. Knowing that without prayer we will lack godliness, God expects us to pray. No matter how weak or strong your prayer life is right now, you can learn to grow even stronger. One of the greatest encouragements to pray is the fact that prayer is answered.

WARM-UP

1. Statistical surveys and experience seem to agree that a large percentage of professing Christians spend little time in sustained prayer, even though they know that prayer is a vital Christian Discipline. Why might this be so?

    ----

2. How do you know when you haven't been praying enough? What are your feelings and concerns during those times?

_____

_____

_____

_____

Prayer Is Expected

I realize that to say prayer is expected of us may make the children of a nonconformist, antiauthoritarian age bristle a bit. Those who have been brought under the authority of Christ and the Bible, however, know that the will of God is for us to pray. But we also believe that His will is good. Furthermore, it is a person—the Lord Jesus Christ, with all authority and with all love—who expects us to pray. These excerpts from His words show that He Himself expects us to pray:

- Matthew 6:5, "And when you pray, . . ."
- Matthew 6:6, "But when you pray, . . ."
- Matthew 6:7, "And when you pray, . . ."
- Matthew 6:9, "Pray then like this: . . ."
- Luke 11:9, "Ask . . . ; seek . . . ; knock."
- Luke 18:1, "And he told them a parable to the effect that they ought always to pray."

The Expectation Is Specific

Colossians 4:2 says, "Continue steadfastly in prayer." When you make something a priority, when you sacrifice for it, when you give time to it, you know you are devoted to it. God expects Christians to be devoted to prayer.

First Thessalonians 5:17 states, "Pray without ceasing." While "continue steadfastly in prayer" emphasizes prayer as an activity, "pray without ceasing" reminds us that prayer is also a relationship. Prayer is in one sense an expression of a Christian's unbroken relationship with the Father. So we must see the expectation to pray not only as a divine summons, but also as a royal invitation. As the writer of Hebrews told us, "Let us then with confidence draw near to the throne of grace, that we may receive mercy and find grace to help in time of need" (4:16).

God also expects us to pray just as a general expects to hear from his soldiers in the battle. One writer reminds us that "prayer is a walkie-talkie for warfare, not a domestic intercom for increasing our conveniences."[1] God expects us to use the walkie-talkie of prayer because that is the means He has ordained not only for godliness, but also for the spiritual warfare between His kingdom and the kingdom of His Enemy. To abandon prayer is to fight the battle with our own resources at best, and to lose interest in the battle at worst.

Moreover, we know this: Jesus prayed. Luke told us, "But he would withdraw to desolate places and pray" (Luke 5:16). If Jesus needed to pray, how much more do we need to pray? Prayer is expected of us because we need it.

Why, then, do so many believers confess that they do not pray as they should? Sometimes the problem is primarily a lack of discipline. Prayer is never planned; time is never allotted just for praying. Often we do not pray because we doubt that anything will actually happen if we pray. Of course, we don't admit this publicly. A lack of sensing the nearness of God may also discourage prayer. When there is little awareness of real need there is little real prayer. Some circumstances drive us to our knees. But there are periods when life seems quite manageable. Although Jesus said, "Apart from me you can do nothing" (John 15:5), this truth hits home more forcefully at some times than at others. When our awareness of the greatness of God and the gospel is dim, our prayer lives will be small. Another reason many Christians pray so little is because they haven't learned about prayer.

Prayer Is Learned

There is a sense in which prayer needs to be taught to a child of God no more than a baby needs to be taught to cry. But crying for basic needs is minimal communication, and we must soon grow beyond that infancy. The Bible says we must pray for the glory of God, in His will, in faith, in the name of Jesus, with persistence, and more. A child of God gradually learns to pray like this in the same way that a growing child learns to talk. Note the ways we learn how to pray.

By praying. If you've ever learned a foreign language, you know that you learn it best when you actually have to speak it. The same is true with the "foreign language" of prayer. The best way to learn how to pray is to pray.

By meditating on Scripture. Meditation is the missing link between Bible intake and prayer. Too often disjointed, the two should be united. At least two Scriptures teach this by example. David prayed in Psalm 5:1, "Give ear to my words, O Lord; consider my groaning." The Hebrew word rendered as "groaning" may also be translated "meditation." In fact, this same word is used with that meaning in another passage, Psalm 19:14: "Let the words of my mouth and the meditation of my heart be acceptable in your sight, O Lord, my rock and my redeemer." Notice that both verses are prayers, pleas to God that consisted of David's "words" (as we'd expect in prayer), but they also involved "meditation." In each case, meditation was a catalyst that catapulted David from considering the truth of God into talking with God.

The process works like this: After the input of a passage of Scripture, meditation allows us to take what God has said and think deeply on it, digest it, and then speak to God about it in meaningful prayer. As a result, we pray about what we've encountered in the Bible, now personalized through meditation. And not only do we have something substantial to say in prayer, as well as the confidence that we are praying God's thoughts to Him, but we transition smoothly into prayer and with more passion for what we're praying about.

William Bates, a Puritan minister of "distinguished talents and piety,"[2] said, "What is the reason that our desires like an arrow shot by a weak bow do not reach the mark? but only this, we do not meditate before prayer. . . . The great reason why our prayers are ineffectual, is because we do not meditate before them."[3]

By praying with others. The disciples learned to pray, not only by hearing Jesus teach about prayer, but also by being with Him when He prayed. In a similar way, we can learn to pray by praying with other people who can model true prayer for us. We pray with them to learn principles of prayer, not to pick up new words and phrases for prayer.

By reading about prayer. Reading about prayer instead of praying simply will not do. But reading about prayer in addition to praying enriches your education in prayer. Reading the books of wise men and women of prayer gives us the privilege of "walking" with them and learning the insights God gave them on how to pray.

Let me add a word of encouragement. No matter how difficult prayer seems for you now, if you will persevere in learning how to pray you can enjoy the hope of an even stronger and more fruitful prayer life ahead of you.

Prayer Is Answered

I love how David addressed the Lord in Psalm 65:2: "O you who hear prayer." Perhaps no principle of prayer is more taken for granted than this one—that prayer is answered. Try to read this promise of Jesus as though it were for the first time: "Ask, and it will be given to you; seek, and you will find; knock, and it will be opened to you. For everyone who asks receives, and the one who seeks finds, and to the one who knocks it will be opened" (Matthew 7:7-8). Since God answers prayer, when we "ask and receive not" we must consider the possibility, as Andrew Murray put it, that "there is something amiss or wanting"[4] in our prayer.

God doesn't mock us with His promises to answer prayer. He does not lead us to pray in order to frustrate us by slamming heaven's door in our face. Let's discipline ourselves to pray and to learn about prayer so that we may be more like Jesus in experiencing the joy of answered prayer.

Prayerful people become godly people, for prayerfulness with God cultivates godliness in all of life. My ministerial experience concurs with the words of J. C. Ryle: "What is the reason that some believers are so much brighter and holier than others? . . . I believe that those who are not eminently holy pray *little*, and those who are eminently holy pray *much*."[5] Would you be like Christ? Then do as He did—discipline yourself to be a person of prayer. (Taken from chapter 4 of *Spiritual Disciplines for the Christian Life*.)

God Expects Us to Pray

3. What do Matthew 6:5-7,9; Luke 11:9; and 18:1 teach about Jesus' view of prayer?

   _____

   _____

   _____

4. How might you apply Colossians 4:2 and 1 Thessalonians 5:17 in the midst of your busy schedule?

   _____

   _____

   _____

5. First Thessalonians 5:17 tells Christians to "pray without ceasing." *Spiritual Disciplines for the Christian Life*, page 82, says that "praying without ceasing means you never really stop conversing with God; you simply

have frequent interruptions." Do you agree with this definition? Why or why not?

6. Have you ever felt that prayer was more *obligation* than *opportunity*? If so, why? If not, why not?

7. Why did Jesus pray in "desolate places" (Luke 5:16)?

8. Describe a time when God answered your specific prayer.

9. Why should our praying be governed by the truth of Scripture rather than by our feelings?

Prayer Is Learned

10. Has anyone ever taught you about prayer? If so, who? If not, who might you seek out to teach you?

11. What role, according to John 16:13, does the Holy Spirit play in your prayer life?

12. How would you describe the relationship between biblical meditation and prayer? (See Psalm 5:1; 19:14, and reread the quote by William Bates on page 43.)

13. a. Thomas Manton, a Puritan preacher, wrote, "It is rashness to pray and not to meditate. What we take in by the word we digest by meditation and let out by prayer."[6] What is your response to this thought?

b. Why do you think more churches today don't teach about the relationship between meditation and prayer?

---

c. How has this lack of teaching affected the church as a whole? Your life? The lives of others you know?

---

14. What is the difference between learning "principles of prayer" and learning "phrases for prayer"?

---

15. What book(s) on prayer have you or others in the group found helpful? In what ways?

God Answers Prayer

16. Read Matthew 7:7-8 again. Discuss the following phrases:

"Ask, and it will be given to you."
"Seek, and you will find."
"Knock, and it will be opened to you."
"For everyone who asks receives."
"The one who seeks finds."
"To the one who knocks it will be opened."

17. a. Andrew Murray wrote, "If you ask and receive not, it must be because there is something amiss or wanting in the prayer." Do you agree with this statement? Explain.

_____

_____

_____

_____

b. Discuss how the following may affect answers to prayer:

Impatience/lack of perseverance in prayer
Selfish motives
Unrepentant sin in your life
Unwillingness to accept that God may answer in ways that are not obvious
Asking for things that are outside the will of God or don't glorify Him

CLOSING PRAYER

Thank the Lord that He not only hears your prayers but also desires them because He longs to develop a deeper relationship with you. Ask Him to draw you deeper into disciplined prayer, to teach you what it means to "pray without ceasing," and to show you how biblical meditation can strengthen your Bible intake and prayers.

GOING DEEPER

(Extra questions for further study)

18. a. At which times in your life have you felt that prayer didn't work, that God wasn't listening?

    _____

    _____

    _____

    b. How does what you've learned in this session relate to this situation?

    _____

    _____

    _____

19. Does persistent prayer tend to develop deeper gratitude toward God? Faith in God? Explain your answers. (See Matthew 7:7-8; Luke 18:1-8.)

    _____

    _____

    _____

    _____

20. In what ways does the Enemy sidetrack your prayer life?
Be specific.

_____

_____

_____

21. What do you think is the relationship between a Christian's
view of God's willingness and ability to answer prayer,
the person's love for God, and his or her willingness to
persevere in prayer?

_____

_____

_____

22. Think about a time when you experienced the joy of
answered prayer. What did you learn during that time
that you might apply to your situation today?

_____

_____

_____

23. If we do not persevere in prayer, what are we demonstrating that we believe about God's love for us? About His
promises to us?

_____

_____

_____

24. This week, plan to link your Bible reading to prayer through biblical meditation. Share your experiences with the group when you meet again.

_____

_____

_____

_____

_____

WORSHIP . . .
FOR THE PURPOSE OF GODLINESS

CENTRAL IDEA

Worship—focusing on and responding to God—is the duty and privilege of all people. Worship usually includes words and actions but goes beyond them to the focus of our hearts and minds. God expects us to worship Him, our Creator, in spirit and according to the truth of Scripture. We cannot become godly without worshipping Him, but it is possible to worship Him in vain (see Matthew 15:8-9). As we learn the Spiritual Discipline of worship, we will become more like Jesus and understand and appreciate how worthy He is of our worship.

WARM-UP

1. What thoughts does the word *worship* bring to your mind? Is the connotation positive or negative? Why?

....

....

....

2. Think about a time when you really felt close to God in worship. What do you think made that time so meaningful? If you feel comfortable doing so, share this with the group.

_____

_____

_____

_____

Jesus Himself reemphasized and obeyed the Old Testament command, "Worship the Lord your God" (Matthew 4:10). It is the duty (and privilege) of all people to worship their Creator. "Oh come, let us worship and bow down," says Psalm 95:6, "let us kneel before the LORD, our Maker!" God clearly expects us to worship. It's our purpose! Godliness without the worship of God is unthinkable. But those who pursue godliness must realize that it is possible to worship God in vain. Jesus quoted another Old Testament passage to warn of worshipping God vainly: "This people honors me with their lips, but their heart is far from me; in vain do they worship me" (Matthew 15:8-9).

How can we worship God without worshiping Him in vain? We must learn an essential part of pursuing Christlikeness—the Spiritual Discipline of worship.

Worship Is . . . Focusing on and Responding to God

To worship God means to ascribe the proper worth to God, to magnify His worthiness of praise, or better, to approach and address God as He is worthy. He is worthy of all the worth and honor we can give Him and then infinitely more. Notice, for instance, how those around the throne of God in Revelation 4:11 and 5:12 address God as "worthy" of so many things.

The more we focus on God, the more we understand and

appreciate His infinite worth. As we understand and appreciate this, we can't help but respond to Him. Just as an indescribable sunset or a breathtaking mountaintop vista evokes a spontaneous response, so we cannot encounter the worthiness of God without the response of worship. If you could see God at this moment, you would so utterly understand how worthy He is of worship that you would instinctively fall on your face and worship Him. And to the degree we truly comprehend more of God, we will in turn respond to Him more in worship.

That's why all the worship of God—public, family,[1] and private worship—should be based upon and include the Bible, because it reveals God to us so that we may focus on Him. Bible reading and preaching are central in public worship because they are the clearest, most direct, most extensive presentation of God in the gathering. For the same reasons, Bible intake and meditation are the heart of private worship.

Worship usually includes words and actions, but it goes beyond them to the *focus* of the mind and heart. Worship is the God-centered focus and response of the soul; it is being preoccupied with God. Since worship is focusing on and responding to God, regardless of what else we are doing we are not worshipping if we are not thinking about God. No matter what you are saying or singing or doing at any moment, you are worshipping God only when He is the center of your attention.

Worship Is . . . Done in Spirit and Truth

Before we can worship in spirit and truth we must have within us the One who is the "Spirit of truth" (John 14:17), that is, the Holy Spirit. He lives only within those who have come to Christ in repentance and faith. Without Him true worship will not happen. Having the Holy Spirit residing within does not guarantee that we always *will* worship in spirit and truth, but His presence does mean we *can*.

To worship God in spirit is to worship from the inside out. It also necessitates sincerity in our acts of worship. No matter how spiritual the song you are singing, no matter how poetic the prayer you are praying, if it isn't sincere then it isn't worship, it's hypocrisy.

The balance to worshipping in spirit is to worship in truth. Worship in truth is worship according to the truth of Scripture. We worship God as He is revealed in the Bible, not as we might want Him to be. We worship Him according to the truth of who He says He is. Worship according to the truth of Scripture also means to worship God in the ways to which He has given His approval in Scripture. In other words, we should do in the worship of God what God says in the Bible we should do in worship.

So we must worship in both spirit and truth, with both heart and head, with both emotion and thought. If we worship with too much emphasis on spirit we will be mushy and weak on the truth, worshipping mainly according to feelings. That can lead anywhere from a lazy, unthinking tolerance of anything in worship at one extreme to uncontrollable spiritual wildfire on the other. But if we overemphasize worship in truth and minimize worship in spirit, then our worship will be taut, grim, and icily predictable.

Worship Is . . . Expected, Both Publicly and Privately

According to Hebrews 10:25, God expects His people to participate regularly in worship gatherings with other believers, warning specifically about "not neglecting to meet together, as is the habit of some."

The church of Jesus Christ is not a collection of isolationists. The New Testament describes the church with metaphors like "flock" (Acts 20:28), "body" (1 Corinthians 12:12), "structure" (Ephesians 2:21), and "household" (Ephesians 2:19), each of which implies a relationship between individual units and a larger whole.

Furthermore, the blessing of a consistent, high-quality, personal devotional life doesn't exempt you from worshipping with other believers. Your devotional experiences may rival those of Jonathan Edwards or George Müller, but you need corporate worship as much as they and these Jewish Christians in Hebrews 10:25 did. There's an element of worship and the Christian life that can never be experienced in private worship or by watching worship.

On the other hand, no matter how fulfilling or sufficient our regular public worship celebration seems, there are experiences with God that He gives only in our private worship. Jesus participated faithfully in the public worship of God at the synagogue each Sabbath (see Luke 4:16) and at the stated assemblies of Israel at the temple in Jerusalem. In addition to that, however, Luke observed that Jesus "would withdraw to desolate places and pray" (5:16). As the familiar Puritan commentator Matthew Henry put it, "Public worship will not excuse us from secret worship."[2]

We must not forget, however, that God expects us to worship privately so He can bless us. We minimize our joy when we neglect the daily worship of God in private. Think of it: The Lord Jesus Christ stands ready to meet with you privately for as long as you want; willing—even eager—to meet with you every day!

Worship Is . . . a Discipline to Be Cultivated

Jesus said, "Worship the Lord your God" (Matthew 4:10). To worship God throughout a lifetime requires discipline. Without discipline, our worship of God will be thin and inconsistent.

Certainly, though, worship must be much more than discipline, more than simply the proper expression of the correct words and forms. True worship also exudes evidence of "heartprints." Worship can't be calculated or produced. Instead it is evoked; it's the response of a heart evoked by the beauty, glory, and allure of the object of your mental focus—Holy God. And yet, we also must be able to consider worship a Discipline, a Discipline that must be cultivated, just as all relationships must be in order for them to remain healthy and grow.

Worship is a Spiritual Discipline insofar as it is both an end and a means. The worship of God is an end in itself because to worship, as we've defined it, is to focus on and respond to God. There is no higher goal or greater spiritual pleasure than focusing on and responding to God. But worship is also a means in the sense that it is a means to godliness. The more we truly worship God, the more—through and by means of worship—we become like Him.

The worship of God makes believers more godly because people become like their focus. We emulate what we think about. If we would be godly, we must focus on God. Godliness requires disciplined worship. (Taken from chapter 5 of *Spiritual Disciplines for the Christian Life*.)

Worship Is . . . Focusing on and Responding to God

3. Do you agree that "Godliness without the worship of God is unthinkable"? Why or why not?

_____

_____

_____

_____

4. Describe what it means to worship God in vain. (See Matthew 15:8-9.)

_____

_____

_____

5. What do the following passages reveal about worship: John 20:28; Revelation 4:8; 5:12-13?

_____

_____

_____

6. According to the following verses, in what ways has God revealed Himself to us so that we might focus on Him?

   John 1:1,14; Hebrews 1:1-2 _____

   _____

   _____

   Romans 1:20 _____

   _____

   _____

   2 Timothy 3:16; 2 Peter 1:20-21 _____

   _____

   _____

Worship Is . . . Done in Spirit and Truth

7. What does John 4:23-24 reveal about how God desires His people to worship?

   _____

   _____

   _____

8. What do you think this text means: "To worship God in spirit is to worship from the inside out"?

   _____

   _____

   _____

   _____

9. What is the difference between worshipping God as He is revealed in the Bible and worshipping Him as you might want Him to be?

10. One pastor has written, "Where feelings for God are dead, worship is dead."[3] Why is spontaneous affection of the heart so vital to genuine worship?

11. When you don't have the feelings of worship, does that mean you should stop engaging in forms of worship? Why or why not?

12. How can you "delight yourself in the LORD" in your worship (Psalm 37:4)?

13. What are the dangers of worshipping just by feelings? Just by truth?

Worship Is . . . Expected, Both Publicly and Privately

14. a. What is God's view of corporate worship? (See Hebrews 10:25.)

    b. How does this verse conflict with the common assumption that religion is an individual matter only?

15. Consider carefully the comment by Geoffrey Thomas: "There is no way that those who neglect secret worship can know communion with God in the public services of the Lord's Day."[4] Do you agree with this statement? Why or why not?

16. What happens in your life when you neglect the daily worship of God in private?

_____

_____

_____

17. What does Christ's willingness to meet with us privately in worship at any time reveal about His character?

_____

_____

_____

Worship Is . . . a Discipline to Be Cultivated

18. In what ways is it difficult to ask others for help in developing godliness through public and private worship?

_____

_____

_____

19. Can you identify with the quote on page 115 of *Spiritual Disciplines for the Christian Life*: "He worships his work, works at his play, and plays at his worship"? If so, which part(s) do you identify with? Be honest. How might your view of worship be improved?

_____

_____

_____

_____

20. Why do you think it seems easier to worship God one day a week instead of worshipping Him seven days a week? Is one-day-a-week worship even possible? Explain your answer.

_____

_____

_____

CLOSING PRAYER

Focus your mind and heart on the worthiness of God and praise Him for who He is. Thank Him for His willingness to meet with you in worship every day. Focus on His character as revealed in Scripture and respond to Him sincerely. Allow yourself to be fully preoccupied with Him. Allow your deep feelings for Him to well up within you and let them out through praise and adoration.

GOING DEEPER

(Extra questions for further study)

21. What steps can you take this week to improve your private worship? Your public worship?

_____

_____

22. What can you do today to use the means by which God has revealed Himself and thereby focus more fully on and enjoy God?

_____

_____

_____

23. Many Christians believe they have "worshipped" if they merely attend church on Sunday. How does what you've learned in this session expand this perspective of worship?

_____

_____

_____

_____

24. The waters of worship should never stop flowing from our hearts because God is always God and always worthy of worship. If you are not already doing so, how can you channel and distill the flow of your worship into a daily and distinct worship experience?

_____

_____

_____

_____

EVANGELISM . . .
FOR THE PURPOSE OF GODLINESS

CENTRAL IDEA

Evangelism is a natural overflow of the Christian life, but it is also a Discipline. Although all Christians are not expected to use the same methods of evangelism, all Christians are expected to evangelize. Godliness requires that we discipline ourselves in the practice of evangelism. The reason many of us don't witness in effective ways is our lack of discipline.

WARM-UP

1. What images does the word *evangelism* bring to mind?

    _____

    _____

2. Why does God command us to evangelize?

    _____

    _____

    _____

3. Why do you think many Christians are afraid to
    evangelize? What are your fears about evangelism?

_____

_____

_____

_____

Only the sheer rapture of being lost in the worship of God is as exhilarating and intoxicating as telling someone about Jesus Christ. Yet nothing causes an eye-dropping, foot-shuffling anxiety more quickly among a group of Christians like myself than talking about our responsibility to evangelize. In fact, I'm sure I don't know a single Christian who would boldly say, "I am as evangelistic as I should be."

The main idea I want to communicate is that godliness requires that we discipline ourselves in the practice of evangelism. The reason many of us don't witness for Christ in ways that would be effective and relatively fear-free is simply because we don't discipline ourselves to do it.

Evangelism Is Expected

Jesus does not expect all Christians to use the same *methods* of evangelism, but He does expect all Christians to evangelize. Before we go further, let's define our terms. What is evangelism? If we want to define it thoroughly, we could say that *evangelism* is presenting Jesus Christ in the power of the Holy Spirit to sinful people, in order that they may come to put their trust in God through Him, to receive Him as their Savior, and serve Him as their King in the fellowship of His church.[1]

If we want something more concise, we could define New Testament evangelism as communicating the gospel. Anyone faithfully relating the essential elements of God's salvation through Jesus

Christ is evangelizing. Evangelism occurs whether the words of the gospel are spoken, written, or recorded; delivered to one person or to a crowd.

Why is evangelism expected? The Lord Jesus Christ Himself has commanded us to witness. Consider His authority in the following: "Go therefore and make disciples of all nations, baptizing them in the name of the Father and of the Son and of the Holy Spirit, teaching them to observe all that I have commanded you. And behold, I am with you always, to the end of the age" (Matthew 28:19-20). Again Jesus said, "Peace be with you. As the Father has sent me, even so I am sending you" (John 20:21).

These commands weren't given to the apostles only. For example, those of us in the United States can say that the apostles never came to *this* nation, and the apostles will never come to your home, your neighborhood, or to the place where you work. For the Great Commission to be fulfilled there, for Christ to have a witness in that "remote part" of the earth, a Christian like you must discipline yourself to do it.

Evangelism Is Empowered

If it is so obvious to almost all Christians that we are to evangelize, how come almost all Christians seem to disobey that command so often? Some believe that they need months of specialized training to witness effectively. They fear speaking with someone about Christ until they feel confident in the amount of their Bible knowledge and their ability to deal with any potential question or objection.

That confident day, however, never comes. Sometimes we fail to speak of Christ because we are afraid that people will think us strange and reject us. In some cases we can trace our evangelophobia to the method of witnessing we're asked to use. If it requires approaching someone we've never met and striking up a conversation about Christ, most people will be terrified and indicate it by their absence. I think the seriousness of evangelism is the main reason it frightens us. We realize that in talking with someone about Christ, heaven and hell are at stake. The eternal destiny of the person looms before us. Many Christians feel too unprepared for such a challenge.

What is success in evangelism? When the person you witness to comes to Christ? Certainly that's what we want to happen. But if we measure evangelistic success only by conversions, are we failures whenever we share the gospel and people refuse to believe? Was Jesus an "evangelistic failure" when people like the rich young ruler turned away from Him and His message (see Mark 10:21-22)? Obviously not.

We need to learn that sharing the gospel *is* successful evangelism. We ought to have an obsession for souls and tearfully plead with God to see more people converted, but only God can produce the fruit of evangelism called conversion. In this regard we are like the postal service. They measure success by the careful and accurate delivery of the message, not by the response of the recipient. Whenever we share the gospel (which includes the summons to repent and believe), we have succeeded. In the truest sense, *all* biblical evangelism is successful evangelism, regardless of the results.

The power of evangelism is the Holy Spirit. From the instant that He indwells us He gives us the power to witness. Jesus stressed this in Acts 1:8. The Spirit does not empower all Christians to evangelize in the same way; rather all believers have been given power to be witnesses of Jesus Christ. And the evidence that you've been given the power to witness is a changed life. The same Holy Spirit power that changed your life for Christ is the power to witness for Christ. So if God by His Spirit has transformed your life into a follower of Jesus, be confident of this: God has given you Acts 1:8 power. But realize also that the Holy Spirit may grant much power to your witness in an evangelistic encounter without giving to you any *feeling* or *sense* of power in it.

We can be confident that some will believe if we will faithfully and tenaciously share the gospel. The *gospel* is the power of God for salvation and not our own eloquence or persuasiveness. God has His elect whom He will call and whom He has chosen to call *through the gospel* (see Romans 8:29-30; 10:17).

Living a life openly devoted to Christ also manifests a power that augments evangelism. Paul described the power of godliness in 2 Corinthians 2:14-17, which says that the Lord empowers the life and the words of the faithful believer with a power of spiritual attraction, making him or her like a fragrant aroma that attracts people to the message about His Son. The most powerful ongoing Christian witness has always been the speaking of God's Word by one who is living God's Word.

Evangelism Is a Discipline

Evangelism is a natural overflow of the Christian life. Every Christian should be able to talk about what the Lord has done for him and what He means to her. But evangelism is also a *Discipline* in that we must discipline ourselves to get into situations where evangelism can occur; that is, we must not just wait for witnessing opportunities to happen.

Jesus said in Matthew 5:16, "Let your light shine before others, so that they may see your good works and give glory to your Father who is in heaven." Any Christian who has heard biblical preaching, participated in Bible studies, and has read the Scriptures and Christian literature for any time at all should have at least enough understanding of the basic message of Christianity to share it with someone else. Even so, many Christians don't actively witness.

Isn't the main reason we don't witness the simple lack of *disciplining* ourselves to do it? Yes, there are those wonderful, unplanned opportunities God appoints to give the "reason for the hope that is in you" (1 Peter 3:15). Nevertheless, I maintain that apart from making evangelism a Spiritual Discipline, most Christians will seldom share the gospel. So, the point is not so much how many unbelievers you see every day, but how often you are with them in an appropriate context for sharing the gospel. Despite the important work-related discussions you may have throughout the day, how often do you have the kinds of meaningful conversations with co-workers where spiritual issues can be raised?

That's why I say evangelism is a Spiritual Discipline. Unless we discipline ourselves for evangelism, we can easily excuse ourselves from ever sharing the gospel with anyone. You'll have to discipline yourself to ask your neighbors how you can pray for them or when you can share a meal with them. You'll have to discipline yourself to get with your coworkers during off-hours. Many such opportunities for evangelism will never take place if you wait for them to occur spontaneously. The world, the flesh, and the Devil will do their best to see to that. You, however, backed by the invincible power of the Holy Spirit, can make sure that these enemies of the gospel do not win.

Regardless of how shy or unskilled we may feel about evangelism, we must not convince ourselves that we cannot or will not verbally share the gospel. Often it is the message of the Cross *lived* and *demonstrated* that God uses to open a heart to the gospel, but it is the message of the Cross *proclaimed* (by word or page) through which the power of God saves those who believe its content. No matter how well we live the gospel (and we must live it well, else we hinder its reception), sooner or later we must communicate the *content* of the gospel before a person can become a disciple of Jesus. (Taken from chapter 6 of *Spiritual Disciplines for the Christian Life*.)

Evangelism Is Expected

4. According to Acts 1:8, in whose power are we to witness (as opposed to doing it in our own power)?

_____

_____

_____

_____

5. What do the following verses reveal about evangelism?
Luke 24:27 _____

_____

_____

John 20:21 _____

_____

_____

6. Why do you think God commands all His people to evangelize and not just those who find it easy to present themselves and their beliefs to other people?

_____

_____

_____

7. What does 1 Peter 2:9 say about God's people?

_____

_____

_____

Evangelism Is Empowered

8. We read in John 9 about the blind man Jesus healed. What is striking about his words to the Pharisees?

_____

_____

_____

9. According to this John 9 passage, when should we witness?

10. Have you ever been afraid to share Christ? If so, when? Why were you afraid?

11. With which evangelistic approach(es) are you most comfortable? Which ones intimidate you? Be honest.

12. Discuss with your group the kinds of responses—positive and negative—you received when you shared the good news of Christ with others.

13. Researcher George Barna says that most Christians who witness to others come away feeling like failures. So, since they don't like to fail, they redirect their efforts into spiritual activities in which they are more likely to be satisfied and successful.[2] Have you found this to be true? Why or why not?

14. Are you confident that God has given you Acts 1:8 power? Why or why not?

15. What does 2 Corinthians 2:14-17 say about God's power through us? About our impact on non-Christians?

16. What does Colossians 4:5-6 say about how to approach evangelism? Why is such preparation so important?

17. What is your estimate of the number of times you have heard the gospel in your life? In a paragraph or so, write the gospel message a person must hear to be saved. Discuss with your group what is necessary for a presentation of the gospel to be clear and complete.

18. Consider ways you might begin to make evangelism a Spiritual Discipline. What steps can you take this week to build deeper relationships with unbelievers?

19. It is said that every Christian is at every moment a testimony—good or bad—to the power of Jesus Christ. What implications does this truth have in evangelism?

CLOSING PRAYER

Focus on what God has done for you and on the importance of sharing Him with others. Ask the Lord to nurture the Discipline of evangelism this week. Ask Him to guide you to at least one person who is open to the gospel.

GOING DEEPER
(Extra questions for further study)

20. Why is it necessary to communicate the gospel's content in addition to living out its truths daily?

_____

_____

_____

21. Which excuses have you used in order to avoid evangelizing your friends? Neighbors? Coworkers? Family members?

_____

_____

_____

22. Write down the names of two people with whom you want to share Christ soon, perhaps even this week. What loving, sensitive steps are you willing to take in order to seek ways of intentionally sharing Christ with them? A lunch meeting? A home meeting? Other?

_____

_____

_____

23. Part of becoming more Christlike is to seek forgiveness for and to eliminate the sin in our lives that make our words and actions seem inconsistent with our faith.

Which sins in your life are creating an obstacle in your willingness and ability to witness?

_____

_____

_____

_____

24. Do you agree with the text on page 137 of *Spiritual Disciplines for the Christian Life* that "the more Christlike our lives, the more convincing our words about Christ" will be? Answer using an illustration from your life.

_____

_____

_____

_____

_____

SERVING . . .
FOR THE PURPOSE OF GODLINESS

CENTRAL IDEA

To serve the Lord with gladness is every Christian's commission. In God's kingdom, no one is spiritually unemployed or retired. Every believer in Christ is gifted to serve, with the goal of being more like Jesus by means of humbly serving others. If we don't discipline ourselves to serve for the sake of Christ and His kingdom, we'll serve only occasionally or when it's convenient or self-serving. The result will be a quantity and quality of service that we'll regret when the Day of Accountability for our service comes.

WARM-UP

1. What, in your mind, is a servant? Describe the feelings you have about being a servant of Christ and His kingdom. Be honest!

2. Would you agree that most servers receive little appreciation for their efforts? If so, why is this? If not, what type of recognition do they receive?

_____

_____

_____

_____

3. If Jesus were to come back to earth today, what types of ministry service would you wish you had done?

_____

_____

_____

_____

Serving God is not a job for the casually interested. It's costly service. God asks for your life. He requires that service to Him to become a priority, not a pastime.

The ministry of serving may be as public as preaching or teaching, but more often it will be as sequestered as nursery duty. Serving may be as appreciated as a powerful testimony in a worship service, but typically it's as thankless as washing dishes after a church social. Most service, even that which seems the most appealing, we perceive as we would the tip of an iceberg. Only the eye of God sees the larger, hidden part of it.

Serving typically looks as unspectacular as the practical needs it seeks to meet. That's why serving must become a Spiritual Discipline. The flesh connives against its hiddenness and sameness. Two of the deadliest of our sins—sloth and pride—loathe serving.

Not every act of service will, or even should, be disciplined serving. Most of the time, our service should spring simply from our love for God and love for others. But because the Spirit of Jesus within us causes us to yearn to be more like Jesus, and also because of the persistent gravitational tendencies toward selfishness in our hearts, we must also discipline ourselves to serve. And those who do will find serving one of the most sure and practical means of growth in grace.

Every Christian Is Expected to Serve

When we are born again and our sins are forgiven, the blood of Christ cleanses our conscience, according to Hebrews 9:14, in order for us to "serve the living God." Every believer's Bible exhorts him or her to "serve the LORD with gladness" (Psalm 100:2, NASB). God's Word has no place for spiritual unemployment or spiritual retirement or any other description of a professing Christian *not* serving God. Of course, motives matter in the service we offer to God. The Bible mentions at least six motives for serving.

Motivated by obedience. In Deuteronomy 13:4, Moses wrote, "You shall walk after the LORD your God and fear him and keep his commandments and obey his voice, and you shall serve him and hold fast to him." Everything in that verse relates to obedience to God. We should serve the Lord because we want to obey Him.

How can any professing Christian think it acceptable to sit on the spiritual sidelines and watch others do the work of the kingdom? Any true Christian would say that he or she *wants* to obey God. But we disobey God when we do not actively serve Him. We sin when we refuse to serve God.

Motivated by gratitude. The prophet Samuel exhorted the people of God to service with these words: "Only fear the LORD and serve him faithfully with all your heart. For consider what great things he has done for you" (1 Samuel 12:24). When serving God seems like a burden, remembering the "great things he has done for you" vaporizes the burden. He has never done anything greater for anyone, nor could He do anything greater for you, than what He has done in bringing you to Himself. If we cannot be grateful servants of Him who is everything and in whom we have everything, what *will* make us grateful?

Motivated by gladness. The inspired command of Psalm 100:2 is, "Serve the LORD with gladness!" God expects His servants to serve—not grudgingly, grimly, or glumly—but gladly.

A believer does not look upon serving God as a burden, but as a privilege. I can understand why the person who serves God in an attempt to earn his way to heaven doesn't serve with gladness. But the Christian who gratefully acknowledges what God has done for him or her for eternity should be able to serve God cheerfully and with joy.

Motivated by forgiveness, not guilt. In Isaiah's famous vision of God, he became eager to serve the Lord once his sins were forgiven (see Isaiah 6:6-8). Like a dog on a leash, Isaiah was straining out of his skin to serve God in some way, *any* way. Because he felt guilty? No! Because God had taken his guilt *away*!

The people of God do not serve Him in order to *be* forgiven but because we *are* forgiven. When believers serve only because they feel guilty, they serve with a ball and chain dragging from their hearts. There's no love in that kind of service, only labor. No one feels joy in it, only obligation and drudgery. Christians should not act like grudging prisoners, sentenced to serve in God's kingdom because of guilt. We can serve willingly because Christ's death freed us from guilt.

Motivated by humility. Jesus was the perfect Servant. With astonishing humility, Jesus, their Lord and Teacher, washed His disciples' feet as an example of how all His followers should serve with humility.

In this world, Christians will always live with an affinity for sin (the Bible calls it the "flesh") that will say, "If I have to serve, I want to get something for it." But this isn't Christlike service. This is hypocrisy. By the power of the Holy Spirit we must reject this self-righteous, hypocritical service as a sinful motivation, and serve "in humility," considering "others more significant" than ourselves (Philippians 2:3).

Motivated by love. At the heart of service, according to Galatians 5:13, should be love: "For you were called to freedom, brothers. Only do not use your freedom as an opportunity for the flesh, but through love serve one another." No fuel for service burns longer and provides more energy than love.

Jesus said in Mark 12:28-31 that the greatest command is to love God with all you are, and the next most important one is to love your neighbor as you love yourself. In light of these words, surely the more we love God the more we will live for Him and serve Him, and the more we love others the more we will serve them.

Every Christian Is Gifted to Serve

At the moment of salvation when the Holy Spirit comes to live within you, He brings a gift with Him. We read in 1 Corinthians 12:4,11 of different varieties of gifts, and we see that the Holy Spirit determines by His sovereign will which gift goes to which believer. Equally important, 1 Peter 4:10 certifies that each Christian receives a special gift, a gift intended for use in service.

Perhaps you have heard little about spiritual gifts, or for whatever reason never identified your spiritual gift. Relax. Many Christians serve God faithfully and fruitfully for a lifetime without ascertaining their specific gift. I'm not suggesting you shouldn't try to discover your gift; I'm saying that you aren't relegated to bench-warmer status in the kingdom of God until you can name your gift.

By all means, don't be discouraged from serving. I encourage you to discipline yourself to serve in a regular, ongoing ministry in your local church. You don't necessarily have to serve in a recognized or elected position. But find a way to defeat the temptation to serve only when it's convenient or exciting. That's not disciplined service.

Serving Is Often Hard Work

Some teach that once you discover and employ your spiritual gift, then serving becomes nothing but effortless joy. That's not New Testament Christianity. The apostle Paul wrote in Ephesians 4:12

about "the equipping of the saints for the *work* of service" (NASB, emphasis added). Sometimes serving God and others is nothing less than hard work. Paul described his service to God with these words in Colossians 1:29: "For this I toil, struggling with all his energy that he powerfully works within me." The word *toil* means "to work to the point of exhaustion," while from the Greek word translated "struggling" comes our word *agonize.*

God supplies us with the desire and power to serve Him, then we struggle in service "with all his energy that he powerfully works" in us. True ministry is never forced out by the strength of the flesh. But do not misunderstand: The result of His power working mightily in us frequently feels like "toil." That means when you serve the Lord in a local church or in any type of ministry, it will often be hard. Like Paul, sometimes your service will also be agonizing and exhausting. It will take your time. It will often prove more stressful or less enjoyable than other ways you could invest your life. And if for no other reason, serving God is hard work because it means serving people. Despite all that, remember: Service that costs nothing accomplishes nothing.

Even though serving God can be agonizing and exhausting work, it is also the most *fulfilling and rewarding* kind of work. Note how, despite the frequent weariness, hunger, thirst, pain, and inconvenience, Jesus said that the work of serving God was so fulfilling to Him that it was like nourishing, satisfying food: "My food is to do the will of him who sent me and to accomplish his *work*" (John 4:34, emphasis added).

Disciplined service is also the most *enduring* kind of work. Unlike some things we may do, service to God is never valueless. Paul, who agonized to the point of exhaustion while serving God reminded us, "Therefore, my beloved brothers, be steadfast, immovable, always abounding in the work of the Lord, knowing that in the Lord your labor is not in vain" (1 Corinthians 15:58).

Are you willing to serve? Like you, the Israelites knew without a doubt that God *expected* them to serve Him, but Joshua once looked them in the eye and challenged them on their *willingness* to serve: "And if it is evil in your eyes to serve the LORD, choose this day whom you will serve. . . . But as for me and my house, we will serve the LORD" (Joshua 24:15).

The Lord Jesus was always the servant, the servant of all, the servant of servants, *the Servant*. He said, "I am among you as the one who serves" (Luke 22:27). One of the clearest indications that a person has truly believed the gospel of Jesus is that a new, Christlike desire to serve begins to overcome his or her selfish desire to be served. And if gospel-transformed, servant-hearted people are to grow more like Christ, they must discipline themselves to serve as Jesus served. (Taken from chapter 7 of *Spiritual Disciplines for the Christian Life*.)

Every Christian Is Expected to Serve

4. Why, according to Hebrews 9:14, does the blood of Christ cleanse our consciences when we become Christians?

------

5. What does it mean to "serve the LORD with gladness" (Psalm 100:2)?

------

6. What does Psalm 84:10 show us about David's view of service?

------

7. Why should we serve the Lord? (See Deuteronomy 13:4.)

8. The text states, "When serving God seems like a burden, remembering the great things he has done for you vaporizes the burden." What great things has God done for you? Be specific.

9. Read Isaiah 6:6-8. What was Isaiah's response to God? Why?

10. C. H. Spurgeon said in a sermon in 1867, "The child of God works not for life, but from life; he does not work to be saved, he works because he is saved."[1] Describe in your own words what he is saying.

11. What can we learn about humble service from each
    of these passages?

    Mark 12:28-31 _____

    _____

    _____

    John 13:12-16 _____

    _____

    _____

    Philippians 2:3 _____

    _____

    _____

12. Why is it so easy for us to serve people for the wrong
    reasons? If you feel free to do so, share a time when you
    served for the wrong reasons.

    _____

    _____

    _____

    _____

13. What, according to Galatians 5:13, is at the heart of
    disciplined service?

    _____

    _____

    _____

    _____

Every Christian Is Gifted to Serve

14. What do each of the following passages reveal about spiritual gifts: 1 Corinthians 12:4-11,27-31; Ephesians 4:7-13; 1 Peter 4:10-11?

15. What do you consider your gift to be? (Read Romans 12:4-8.) Why?

16. How does Colossians 1:29 apply to the work God may be calling you to do?

17. Do you agree that "service that costs nothing accomplishes nothing"? Explain your answer.

18. What does Jesus call the satisfying work of serving God? (See John 4:34.)

_____

_____

_____

19. a. What promise does God make concerning our service to Him?

1 Corinthians 15:58 _____

_____

_____

Hebrews 6:10 _____

_____

_____

b. Does that mean we'll always see the fruit of our labors? Why or why not?

_____

_____

_____

_____

CLOSING PRAYER

Review the six motives for serving mentioned in this chapter. Then express to God the following. Be honest with Him and ask Him to help you grow in these areas:

- Your desire to obey Him
- Your gratitude for what He has done for you
- Your willingness to serve Him gladly
- Your joy at being forgiven
- Your desire to learn humility
- Your love for Him and your desire to love others

GOING DEEPER

(Extra questions for further study)

20. What can you do to make service for God a greater priority in your daily life?

_____

_____

_____

_____

21. What is the difference between serving someone as an act of love and righteousness and serving someone in order to train yourself away from covetousness, arrogance, envy, possessiveness, or resentment?

_____

_____

_____

_____

22. The text on page 156 of _Spiritual Disciplines for the Christian Life_ says that "worship empowers serving; serving expresses worship." What is the relationship between service, on the one hand, and regular private

and congregational worship on the other? Why are both so intertwined?

_____

_____

_____

_____

_____

STEWARDSHIP . . . FOR THE PURPOSE OF GODLINESS

CENTRAL IDEA

The clock and the dollar greatly influence our lives, so we must consider their role in godly living. God calls us to be disciplined in the use of both our time and our money. The biblically disciplined stewardship of time and money are at the heart of a disciplined spiritual life that leads to Christlikeness.

WARM-UP

1. Why do you think people have difficulty managing their money? Which cultural and personal factors contribute to this difficulty?

    ....

    ....

    ....

    ....

2. Do you often feel that "there aren't enough hours in the day"? What are some of the reasons why people feel so much time pressure?

_____

_____

_____

_____

3. When someone mentions your need to be a better steward of money and time, how do you typically respond?

_____

_____

_____

_____

The Disciplined Use of Time

Godliness is the result of a disciplined spiritual life. But at the heart of a disciplined spiritual life is the disciplined use of time. To be like Jesus, we must see the use of our time as a Spiritual Discipline. Having so perfectly ordered His moments and His days, at the end of His earthly life Jesus was able to pray to the Father, "I glorified you on earth, having accomplished the work that you gave me to do" (John 17:4). Here are ten biblical reasons (many of which were made clear to me in the reading of Jonathan Edwards' sermon on "The Preciousness of Time and the Importance of Redeeming It"[1]) to use time wisely.

Use time wisely "because the days are evil." To use time wisely "because the days are evil" is a curious phrase embedded in the inspired language of the apostle Paul in Ephesians 5:15-16. He may have been referring to the persecution or opposition being experienced by himself or the Ephesian church. In any case, the days are evil still. Even without the kind of persecution or opposition known by the Christians of Paul's day, the world we live in makes it difficult to use time wisely, especially for purposes of biblical spirituality and godliness.

The natural course of our minds, our bodies, our world, and our days leads us toward evil, not toward Christlikeness. *Thoughts* must be disciplined, otherwise, like water, they tend to flow downhill or stand stagnant. Our *bodies* incline to ease, pleasure, gluttony, and sloth. Unless we practice self-control, our bodies will tend to serve evil more than God. Finally, our *days* are days of active evil because so many temptations and evil forces are so extremely active in our days.

Wise use of time is the preparation for eternity. You must prepare for eternity in time. This means first, that during time (that is, in this life) you must prepare for eternity, for there will be no second chance to prepare once you cross eternity's timeless threshold. Second, it means that you must prepare for eternity before it is too late.

What, then, is more precious than time? As a relatively small rudder determines the direction of a great ocean liner, so that which we do in the small span of time influences all eternity. Come to God in time, and He will bring you to Himself in eternity.

Time is short. Time would not be so precious if we never died. But since we live never more than a breath away from eternity, the way we use our time has eternal significance. Although decades of life might remain, the fact is, "You are a mist that appears for a little time and then vanishes" (James 4:14). Even the longest life is brief in comparison to eternity.

Time is passing. Not only is time short, but what does remain is fleeting. Time is not like a bag of ice in the freezer, out of which you can use a bit when you want and save the rest for later. Instead, time is very much like the sands in an hourglass—what's left is slipping away. If I don't discipline my use of time for the purpose of godliness now, it won't be any easier later.

The remaining time is uncertain. Not only is time short and passing, but we do not even know how short it actually is or how long before it all passes away. That's why the wisdom of Proverbs 27:1 advises, "Do not boast about tomorrow, for you do not know what a day may bring." Obviously, we must make some types of plans as though many more years remain. But a proper recognition of reality calls us to use our time "for the purpose of godliness" as though it were uncertain we would live tomorrow, for that is a very certain uncertainty.

Time lost cannot be regained. Once gone, it is gone forever and can never be regained. God offers you this present time to discipline yourself for the purpose of godliness. Jesus said in John 9:4, "We must work the works of him who sent me while it is day; night is coming, when no one can work." The time for the works of God, that is, godly living, is now, "while it is day."

You are accountable to God for your time. There's hardly a more sobering statement in Scripture than Romans 14:12: "So then each of us will give an account of himself to God." The words "each of us" apply to Christians and non-Christians alike. And though believers will be saved by grace and not by works, once in heaven our reward there will be determined on the basis of our works. The wise response to such truth is to evaluate your use of time now and spend it in a way that you not regret at the Judgment. And if you cannot answer your conscience regarding how you use your time in the growth of Christlikeness now, how will you be able to answer God then?

Time is so easily lost. Except for the "fool," no other character in the book of Proverbs draws the scorn of Scripture like the slothful "sluggard" (see Proverbs 24:33-34; 26:13-14). The reason? His lazy and wasteful use of time.

Time appears so plentiful that losing much of it seems inconsequential. Yet time is infinitely more precious than money because money can't buy time. You can, however, at least mini-mize the loss and waste of time by disciplining yourself for the purpose of godliness.

We value time at death. As the person out of money values it most when it is gone, so do we at death value time most when it is gone. If additional years were given to us at death, they would profit nothing unless we made a change in how we used our time. So the moment to value time is now, and not just at death.

Time's value in eternity. I doubt that in heaven we experience regret, but if we did it would be for not using our earthly time more for the glory of God and for growth in His grace. Hell, by contrast, will howl forever with agonizing laments over time so foolishly squandered. In Luke 16:22-25, the Bible portrays this anguish over a wasted lifetime in the story of the rich man who went to Hades and of Lazarus who went to "Abraham's side." If those in the merciless side of eternity owned a thousand worlds, they would give them all (if they could) for one of our days.

The Disciplined Use of Money

The Bible relates not only the use of time to our spiritual condition, but also our use of money. Why does God consider a biblical use of our money and resources a crucial part of our growth in godliness? For one thing it's a matter of sheer obedience. A surprisingly large amount of Scripture speaks to the use of wealth and possessions. If we ignore it or take it lightly, our "godliness" will be a fraud. But as much as anything else, the reason our use of money, and the things it buys, indicates our spiritual maturity and godliness is because we exchange such a great part of our lives for it. Because we invest most of our days working in exchange for money, in a very real sense our money represents *us*. Therefore, how we use it reveals who we are, for it manifests our priorities, our values, and our hearts. Growth in godliness will express itself in a growing understanding of these ten New Testament principles of giving.

God owns everything you own. In 1 Corinthians 10:26, the

apostle Paul quoted Psalm 24:1, which reads, "The earth is the Lord's, and the fullness thereof." God owns everything, including everything you possess, because He created everything. God wants us to use and enjoy the things He permits us to have, but as stewards of them we must remember they all belong to Him and should be used for His kingdom. So the question is not, "How much of my money should I give to God?" but rather, "How much of God's money should I keep for now?"

Giving is an act of worship. In Philippians 4:18, the apostle Paul thanked the Christians in the Grecian city of Philippi for the financial gift they gave to support his missionary ministry. He called the money they gave "a fragrant offering, a sacrifice acceptable and pleasing to God," comparing it to an Old Testament sacrifice people gave in worship to God. In other words, Paul said that their act of giving to the work of God was an act of worshipping God. Giving is much more than a duty or an obligation; it is an act of worshipping the Lord.

Giving reflects faith in God's provision. The proportion of your income that you give back to God testifies to how much you trust Him to provide for your needs. We will give to the extent that we believe God will provide for us. The greater our faith that God will provide for our needs, the greater will be our willingness to risk giving to Him. And the less we trust God, the less we will give to Him.

Giving should be sacrificial and generous. Giving isn't sacrificial unless you sacrifice to give. Many professing Christians give only token amounts to the work of God's kingdom. A much smaller number give well. Perhaps only a few actually give sacrificially. Polls consistently show that the more money Americans make, the less sacrificially we give.[2]

I've never known people who gave sacrificially—whether through a one-time sacrificial gift or consistent sacrificial offerings—who regretted it. Sure, they missed having some of the things they could have enjoyed if they'd spent the money on themselves. But the joy and fulfillment they gained by giving away something they could not ultimately keep was more than worth the sacrifice.

Giving reflects spiritual trustworthiness. Jesus revealed this startling insight into the ways of God's kingdom in Luke 16:10-13. If we are not faithful with the money God entrusts to us—and certainly that includes the giving of our money for Christ's kingdom—the Bible says God will deem us untrustworthy to handle spiritual riches.

How you manage the financial "department" of your life is one of the best ways of evaluating your relationship with Christ and your spiritual trustworthiness. If you love Jesus and the work of His kingdom more than anyone or anything, your finances will reflect that. That's why your financial records tell more about you than almost anything else.

Giving—love, not legalism. God does not send you a bill. The church does not send you a bill. We don't give to God and to the support of the work of His kingdom to fulfill some supposed "eleventh commandment." Love to God should motivate giving to God. How much you give should reflect how much you love God. God wants you to give, not as a formality or an obligation, but as the overflow of your love for Him.

Give willingly, thankfully, and cheerfully. "Each one must give as he has decided in his heart, not reluctantly or under compulsion, for God loves a cheerful giver" (2 Corinthians 9:7). God doesn't want you to give with a grudge—that is, you give but you'd rather not. He takes no pleasure in gifts presented resentfully, regardless of the amount you give. He wants you to give because you want to. When you consider how God has given you the greatest possible gift in His Son, Jesus Christ, when you recall the mercy and grace He applies to you, when you reflect on how He provides all you have, and when you remember that you are actually giving to *God*, you should be able to give thankfully and cheerfully.

Giving is an appropriate response to real needs. There are times when genuine needs should be communicated to one's local church, so that the members of the church may give spontaneously in response to those needs. Three instances of this occur in the book of Acts: 2:43-45; 4:32-35; 11:27-30. Notice that no one in these three cases from Acts felt either pressured to give or like they were mandated an amount to give.

We don't have the space to discuss other guidelines for giving in response to special needs, such as making sure you have the necessary facts, confirming the integrity and accountability of those using the money, and so on. But note that despite the biblical legitimacy of spontaneous giving, most of our giving probably should *not* be unplanned.

Giving should be planned and systematic. Notice how the apostle Paul directed the Christians to give in 1 Corinthians 16:1-2: "Now concerning the collection for the saints: as I directed the churches of Galatia, so you also are to do. On the first day of every week, each of you is to put something aside and store it up, as he may prosper, so that there will be no collecting when I come."

Note three observations about this planned, systematic giving. To begin with, Paul told them to give "on the first day of every week." Second, mark that he said "each of you" should do this. All self-identified Christians should express their stewardship of God's money through giving. Third, he said that each is to give "as he may prosper." Generally, the more you prosper, the higher you should make the percentage of your income that you give.

Generous giving results in bountiful blessing. Our Lord Jesus said in Luke 6:38, "Give, and it will be given to you. Good measure, pressed down, shaken together, running over, will be put into your lap. For with the measure you use it will be measured back to you."

God never says that if you give faithfully He will give you a lot of money, or some other specific earthly blessing. But He does say He will bless you in this life if you love and trust Him enough to be generous in your giving to Him. (Taken from chapter 8 of *Spiritual Disciplines for the Christian Life.*)

The Disciplined Use of Time

4. Reread John 17:4. What work do you believe God has given you to do? How well are you completing it?

5. According to Ephesians 5:15-16, "the days are evil." Why, therefore, are we to make the most of our time? How do we do this?

6. Which things hinder you from using your time the way God would have you use it? Be honest.

7. What must you do to obey the command found in Colossians 3:2?

8. How strongly do you believe in the existence of evil spirits today? In what ways does a person's view of evil influence the time he or she spends in the Christian Disciplines?

_____

_____

_____

_____

9. Read 2 Corinthians 6:2 and James 4:14. If you knew you'd be in eternity tomorrow, how would you live life differently today?

_____

_____

_____

10. What circumstances have reminded you that time is passing and death might be near? (See Psalm 31:15.)

_____

_____

_____

11. a. Consider ways in which you've misused time. If you feel comfortable doing so, share them with the group. Also state your most effective means of minimizing the misuse of time.

_____

_____

_____

b. Read Philippians 3:13-14. What is the will of God for us, despite the ways in which we've misused time?

_____

_____

_____

_____

12. What does Hebrews 5:12 say about using our time to gain spiritual maturity?

_____

_____

_____

13. Look up Matthew 12:36 and 25:14-30. What do they say about God's judgment of our actions?

_____

_____

_____

_____

14. What do Proverbs 5:11-13 and 24:33-34 say about lost time and opportunity?

_____

_____

_____

_____

The Disciplined Use of Money

15. Is it easy to grasp that God owns everything we possess? Why or why not?

16. a. What does Luke 16:10-13 say about who God can trust?

    b. Why do you think Luke likens money to a "master" (verse 13)?

17. In what ways can you excel in love by giving? (See 2 Corinthians 8:7.)

18. Why should you give to God willingly, thankfully, and cheerfully?

_____

_____

_____

_____

19. If you are meeting in a group, discuss the meaning of each phrase in 2 Corinthians 9:6-8.

_____

_____

_____

CLOSING PRAYER

Thank God for His love, faithfulness, provision, and—most important of all—for giving His Son as a sacrifice for your sins. Ask Him to reveal ways in which you can better use time and money for the purpose of godliness.

GOING DEEPER

(Extra questions for further study)

20. What are the benefits of a systematic giving plan?

_____

_____

_____

21. What specific steps are you willing to take to implement needed changes in your giving?

_____

_____

_____

_____

22. Are you preparing, through your stewardship of time and money, to stand before God and give an account of your use of time and money? Explain your answer.

_____

_____

_____

_____

23. In light of many people's burnout-prone lifestyle, what can you learn from Ecclesiastes 3:1? In which areas of your life are you too rushed and becoming emotionally and physically drained?

_____

_____

_____

_____

_____

Fasting, Silence, and Solitude . . . for the Purpose of Godliness

CENTRAL IDEA

Christians who do not know much about the Discipline of fasting tend to misunderstand and fear it. It's also difficult to go so radically against the mainstream of culture by fasting. Yet purposeful fasting provides strong benefits in the disciplined pursuit of a Christlike life. It is a discipline that Jesus both taught and practiced. Likewise, the Disciplines of silence and solitude, which Jesus practiced, are foreign to many who have learned to be comfortable only with noise and crowds. Yet these Disciplines contribute much to our spiritual growth and development.

WARM-UP

1. Describe what you think fasting means. Include what you consider to be positive and negative aspects of fasting.

   _____

   _____

   _____

2. Describe what you have learned about fasting from other Christians.

---

3. Have you ever chosen to temporarily seek privacy for spiritual purposes? If so, describe what it was like.

FASTING . . . FOR THE PURPOSE OF GODLINESS

Christians in a gluttonous, denial-less, self-indulgent society may struggle to accept and begin the practice of fasting. Few Disciplines go so radically against the flesh and the mainstream of culture as this one. Nevertheless, we dare not overlook its biblical significance. Of course, some people, for medical reasons, cannot fast. But no Christian should ignore fasting's benefits in the disciplined pursuit of a Christlike life.

Fasting Explained

Christian fasting is a believer's voluntary abstinence from food for *spiritual* purposes. Other types of fasting—despite the benefits they may produce for the mind and body—could not be classified as *Christian* fasting, and fasting by a non-Christian obtains no eternal value. It is for *believers* in Christ, for the Discipline must be rooted in a relationship with Christ and practiced with the desire to become more like Christ. Believers should fast according to biblical teaching and with purposes that are God-centered. It is *voluntary* in that fasting should not be coerced. And fasting is more than just the ultimate crash diet for the body; it is *abstinence from food* for *spiritual purposes*. There is a broader, yet often overlooked view of fasting in which, for spiritual purposes, a person abstains from or denies himself the enjoyment of something other than food. So while it's appropriate to speak of fasting from any legitimate freedom, technically the Bible uses the term only in its primary sense, that is, abstinence from food.

To understand fasting for spiritual purposes, realize that the Bible distinguishes between several kinds of fasts.

- A *normal* fast involves abstaining from all food, but not from water. Matthew 4:2 and Luke 4:2 say that after a forty-day fast Jesus was hungry, but they say nothing about thirst. Unless this was a supernatural fast (see below), the body can't go forty days without water.
- A *partial* fast is a limitation of the diet but not abstention from all food. See Daniel 1:12.[1]
- An *absolute* fast is the avoidance of all food and liquid, even water. See Ezra 10:6; Esther 4:16; Acts 9:9.
- The Bible also describes a *supernatural* fast that requires God's supernatural intervention into the bodily processes. See Deuteronomy 9:9.
- A *private* fast is what Jesus meant in Matthew 6:16-18 when He said we should fast in a way not to be noticed by others.
- *Congregational* fasts are the type found in Joel 2:15-16 and Acts 13:2.
- The Bible also speaks of *national* fasts. See 2 Chronicles 20:3; Nehemiah 9:1; Esther 4:16; Jonah 3:5-8.
- God established one *regular* fast in the Old Covenant.

Every Jew was to fast on the Day of Atonement (see Leviticus 16:29-31).

- Finally, the Bible mentions *occasional* fasts. These occur on special occasions as the need arises. Examples of these are found in 2 Chronicles 20:3, Esther 4:16, Matthew 9:15, and Acts 14:23.

Fasting Is Expected

Notice Jesus' words at the beginning of Matthew 6:16-17: "And *when* you *fast.* . . . But *when* you *fast* . . ." (emphasis added). By giving us instructions on what to do and what not to do when we fast, Jesus assumes that we will fast. Plainer still are His words in Matthew 9:14-15: Jesus said that the time would come when His disciples "will fast." That time is now.

Until Jesus, the Bridegroom of the church, returns for His bride, He expects us to fast. He gave us no command regarding how often or how long we should fast, but like the other Spiritual Disciplines, fasting should never devolve into an empty, legalistic routine. God offers to bless us through fasting as often as we desire.

Fasting Is to Be Done for a Purpose

Without a purpose, fasting can be a miserable, self-centered experience about willpower and endurance. Scripture sets forth many purposes for fasting. I've condensed them into ten major categories. Notice that *none* of the purposes is to earn God's favor. It is useless to fast as a way to impress God and earn His acceptance. Faith in the work of Jesus Christ makes us acceptable to God, not our efforts, regardless of our intensity or sincerity.

Having a biblical purpose for your fast may be the single most important concept to take from this chapter. In real life, here's how it works: As you are fasting and your head aches or your stomach growls and you think, *I'm hungry!* your next thought is likely to be something like, *Oh, right—I'm hungry because I'm fasting today.*

Then your next thought *should* be, *And I'm fasting for this purpose:*
_____.

Although the physical discomfort is unpleasant—perhaps even painful—it is important to feel some degree of hunger during your fast.[2] Your hunger helps you, serving as a continual reminder of your spiritual purpose. For instance, if your purpose is to pray for your spouse, then every time your stomach growls or your head aches, your hunger reminds you that you're fasting, which in turn reminds you that you're fasting for the purpose of praying for your spouse—and then you pray. So throughout your fast, every time you feel hunger—whether you are working, driving, talking to someone, sitting at the computer, walking, or whatever—you are reminded of your purpose, in this case to pray for your spouse.

As a Christian then, whenever you fast, you should do so for at least one of these biblical purposes.

To strengthen prayer. There's something about fasting that sharpens the edge of our intercessions and deepens the passion of our supplications. The people of God have frequently utilized fasting when they have felt a special urgency about the concerns they lift before the Father. The Bible does not teach that fasting is a kind of spiritual hunger strike that compels God to do our bidding. If we ask for something outside of God's will, fasting does not cause Him to reconsider. Fasting does not change God's hearing so much as it changes our praying. To see some of the places in Scripture where fasting is connected with prayer, read Ezra 8:23, Nehemiah 1:4, Daniel 9:3, and Acts 13:3.

To seek God's guidance. A second purpose for fasting is to more clearly discern the will of God. (See Judges 20:26-28 and Acts 14:23.) Fasting does not *ensure* the certainty of receiving such clear guidance from God. Rightly practiced, however, it does make us more receptive to the One who loves to guide us.

To express grief. As mentioned in Judges 20:26, one of the reasons the Israelites wept and fasted before the Lord was not only to seek His guidance, but to express grief for the forty thousand brothers they had lost in battle. Grief caused by events other than a death also can be expressed through fasting. Christians have fasted because of grief for their sins and as a means of expressing grief for the sins of others.

To seek deliverance or protection. One of the most common fasts in biblical times was a fast to seek salvation from enemies or circumstances. (Examples of this are found in 2 Chronicles 20:3-4; Ezra 8:21-23; Esther 4:16; and Psalm 109:20-24.) Fasting, rather than fleshly efforts, should be one of our first defenses against "persecution" because of our faith.

To express repentance and the return to God. Fasting for this purpose is similar to fasting for the purpose of expressing grief for sin. See, for instance, 1 Samuel 7:6, Joel 2:12, and Jonah 3:5-8. But as repentance is a change of mind resulting in a change of action, fasting can represent more than just grief over sin. It also can signal a commitment to obedience and a new direction.

To humble oneself before God. Fasting, when practiced with the right motives, is a physical expression of humility before God, just as kneeling or prostrating yourself in prayer can reflect humility before Him. Wicked King Ahab eventually humbled himself before the Lord by means of fasting in 1 Kings 21:27-29 and King David did the same in Psalm 35:13.

To express concern for the work of God. This is illustrated in Nehemiah 1:3-4 and Daniel 9:3. Just as a parent might fast and pray out of concern for the work of God in the life of a child, so Christians may fast and pray because they feel a burden for the work of God on a relatively broad scale. For example, Christians might feel compelled to fast and pray for the work of God in a place that has experienced tragedy, disappointment, or apparent defeat.

To minister to the needs of others. Those who think the Spiritual Disciplines foster tendencies of introspection or independence should consider Isaiah 58. In the most extensive passage in Scripture dealing exclusively with fasting, God emphasizes fasting for the purpose of meeting the needs of others.

To overcome temptation and dedicate yourself to God. Ask Christians to name a fast by a biblical character and most will probably think first of the lengthy fast of Jesus prior to His temptation in Matthew 4:1-11. Sometimes when we struggle with temptation, or when we anticipate grappling with it, we know that we need extra spiritual strength to overcome it. In times of exceptional temptation, exceptional measures are required. One such exceptional measure in your situation might be a Christlike fast for the purpose of overcoming the temptation and of renewing your dedication to God.

To express love and worship to God. Fasting can be a testimony—even one directed to yourself—that you find your greatest pleasure and enjoyment in life from God. It's a way of demonstrating to yourself that you love God more than food, that seeking Him is more important to you than eating, that Jesus—the bread of heaven (see John 6:51)—is more satisfying to you than earthly bread. A woman named Anna expressed her devotion to God in this way according to Luke 2:37.

Fasting is when we hunger for God—for a fresh encounter with God, for God to answer a prayer, for God to save someone, for God to work powerfully in our church, for God to guide us or protect us—more than we hunger for the food God made us to live on.

There is no doubt that God has often crowned fasting with extraordinary blessings. But we should be careful not to develop what Martyn Lloyd-Jones called a mechanical view of fasting. We cannot manipulate God to do our bidding by fasting any more than we can by any other means. As with prayer, we fast in hope that by His *grace* God will bless us as we desire. When our fast is rightly motivated, we can be sure God *will* bless us and do so in the way infinite wisdom knows is best, even if it is not in the way we wanted. Whether or not you receive the specific blessing you seek, one thing is sure: If you knew what God knew, you would give yourself the identical blessing that He does. And none of His rewards are worthless. (Taken from chapter 9 of *Spiritual Disciplines for the Christian Life.*)

SILENCE AND SOLITUDE . . .
FOR THE PURPOSE OF GODLINESS

Explanation of Silence and Solitude

The Discipline of silence is the voluntary and temporary abstention from speaking so that certain spiritual goals might be sought.
Sometimes silence is observed in order to read the Bible, meditate
on Scripture, pray, journal, and so on. Though there is no outward
speaking, there may be intentional, biblical self-talk or prayer to
God. At other times you might choose not to talk at all, but simply
to focus your mind upon God and to "set your minds on things
that are above" (Colossians 3:2), resting your soul in the love He
displayed through Christ.

Solitude is the Spiritual Discipline of voluntarily and temporarily
withdrawing to privacy for spiritual purposes. The period of solitude may last only a few minutes or for days. As with silence, solitude may be sought in order to participate without interruption in
other Spiritual Disciplines, or just to be alone with God and think.

First, think of silence and solitude as complementary Disciplines
to fellowship. Without silence and solitude we can be active, but shal-
low. Without fellowship we can be deep, but stagnant. Christlikeness
requires both sides of the equation. Second, silence and solitude are
usually found together. Though they can be distinguished (as seen
in the definitions above), in this chapter we will think of them as a
pair. Third, recognize that culture conditions us to be comfortable
with noise and crowds, not with silence and solitude.

There are many biblical reasons for making priorities of the
Spiritual Disciplines of silence and solitude:

- To follow Jesus' example. The Scriptures teach that Jesus
  engaged in periods of silence and solitude (see Matthew
  4:1; 14:23; Mark 1:35; Luke 4:42)
- To minimize distractions in prayer. One of the more
  obvious reasons for getting away from the sounds and

surroundings that divert our attention is to better focus the mind in prayer (see 1 Kings 19:8,11-13; Habakkuk 2:1; Galatians 1:17)
- To express worship to God in a way that does not require words, sounds, or actions (see Habakkuk 2:20; Zephaniah 1:7; Zechariah 2:13)
- To express faith in God (see Psalm 62:1-2,5-6; Isaiah 30:15)
- To seek the salvation of the Lord (see Lamentations 3:25-28)
- To be physically and spiritually restored (see Mark 6:31)
- To regain a spiritual perspective (see Luke 1:5-25,57-64)
- To seek the will of God, for at times He discloses it only in private (see Luke 6:12-13)
- To learn control of the tongue (see Proverbs 17:27-28; Ecclesiastes 3:7; James 1:19,26; 3:2; taken from chapter 10 of *Spiritual Disciplines for the Christian Life*)

Fasting Explained

4. List the ten biblical purposes of fasting.

5. Review the various kinds of fasts mentioned in the Bible. Then determine which kind of fast each of the following passages describes:

Deuteronomy 9:9 _____

_____

Ezra 10:6 _____

_____

Esther 4:16 _____

_____

Daniel 1:12 _____

_____

Jonah 3:5-8 _____

_____

Matthew 3:4 _____

_____

Matthew 4:2 _____

_____

Luke 4:2 _____

_____

6. Place the first four biblical purposes of fasting into a group, then the next three, then the last three. Which one from each group do you think would be most common?

_____

_____

_____

7. Consider these passages, noticing the word *when*: Matthew 6:2-3,5-7,16-17. What do they reveal about the importance of fasting?

_____

_____

8. What do we learn about fasting from Matthew 9:14-15?

_____

_____

9. What specific instructions about fasting are given in Matthew 6:16-18?

_____

_____

_____

Fasting Is to Be Done for a Purpose

10. Why is having a biblical purpose for your fast perhaps "the single most important concept to take from this chapter"?

_____

_____

_____

11. How does some degree of hunger actually help you during a fast? When you sense hunger during a fast, what is the mental process it should trigger?

_____

_____

_____

12. Read Ezra 7:11-20; 8:21-23. What was Ezra's situation, and what did he do?

_____

_____

_____

13. God is always pleased to hear His people's prayers and is also pleased when we choose to strengthen our prayers through fasting. Why did the following people fast?

    Nehemiah (see Nehemiah 1:3-4) _____

    _____

    _____

    The early Christians (see Acts 13:2-3) _____

    _____

    _____

14. What is the relationship between repentance and fasting? (See 1 Samuel 7:6; Joel 2:12; Jonah 3:5-8.)

    _____

    _____

    _____

15. What does Isaiah 58:6-7 reveal about the role of fasting in meeting the needs of others?

Explanation of Silence and Solitude

16. Look up these verses: Matthew 4:1; 14:23; Mark 1:35; Luke 4:42. What do they tell us about Jesus?

17. Why do you think many of us are uncomfortable when we are alone with our own thoughts and God's Word?

18. Read Mark 6:31. Do you receive enough rest? What steps can you take to have time alone with God to restore your body and spirit?

19. In which area(s) do you need to seek God's will? What can you learn from Jesus' actions in Luke 6:12-13?

_____

_____

_____

_____

CLOSING PRAYER

Psalm 62:1-2,5-6 contains some beautiful phrases that relate to our faith. Read these verses and write out your thoughts in the form of a prayer. If you, or others, are comfortable praying aloud, do so.

GOING DEEPER

(Extra questions for further study)

20. Are you willing to put aside your physical needs in order to seek God? Why or why not?

_____

_____

_____

21. Fasting can be little more than a dead work if we persistently harden our hearts to God's call to deal with a specific sin in our lives. What sin in your life do you need to deal with today?

_____

_____

_____

22. Consider the following ways you can make silence and solitude more of a reality and a habit. Which will you pursue this coming week?

   • Looking to Christ during various "minute retreats" each day as you "improve" a minute of waiting at a traffic signal, for an elevator, at a drive-through, and so on
   • Developing a daily time of Bible intake and prayer when you're alone with God
   • Experiencing extended periods of silence and solitude—an afternoon, evening, or weekend
   • Locating special places where you can apply the Disciplines of silence and solitude—a park, by a stream, in a special room at home, at church, or elsewhere
   • Arranging to trade off responsibilities with your spouse or a friend so you can each have some time alone with God

JOURNALING AND LEARNING . . . FOR THE PURPOSE OF GODLINESS

CENTRAL IDEA

Although journaling is not commanded in Scripture, something very much like what we call journaling is modeled there in Psalms and in Jeremiah's Lamentations. God has blessed the use of journals since biblical times. Keeping a spiritual journal can be a valuable aid to maintaining other Spiritual Disciplines, such as biblical meditation. Although there are no rules for keeping a journal and journaling can be fruitful at any level of involvement, journaling requires persistence through the dry times. Its value can be experienced only through doing it.

Godly learning is an important Spiritual Discipline because the more Christlike we grow, the more we will pursue a full head as well as a full heart. As Proverbs 9:9 tells us, a characteristic of wise people is their desire for godly learning. We must not be content to have zeal for God without knowledge. Jesus Himself said to "love the Lord your God . . . with all your mind" (Mark 12:29-30). We glorify God when we use our minds as well as our hearts to learn of Him, His ways, His Word, and His world.

WARM-UP

1. Is your impression of journaling positive or negative? What has helped to shape this impression?

_____

_____

_____

_____

2. Why is it important for Christians to continue to learn about God? About the world? About themselves?

_____

_____

_____

_____

JOURNALING . . . FOR THE PURPOSE OF GODLINESS

Journaling has a fascinating appeal with nearly all who hear about it. One reason is the way journaling blends the Bible and daily living, like the confluence of two great rivers into one.

Explanation of Journaling

As a Christian, your journal is a place to document the works and ways of God in your life. Your journal also can include an account of daily events, a record of personal relationships, a notebook of insights into Scripture, and/or a list of prayer requests. Spontaneous devotional thoughts or lengthy theological musings can also be preserved there.

A journal is one of the best places for charting your progress in the other Spiritual Disciplines and for holding yourself accountable to your goals. Woven throughout this fabric of entries and events are the colorful strands of your reflections and feelings about them. How you respond to these matters, and how you interpret them from your own spiritual perspective, express the heart of journaling.

Does a Christian have to keep a journal in order to grow more like Jesus Christ? No, nothing in Scripture obligates the followers of Jesus to keep a journal. On the one hand, unlike prayer, the practice of journaling certainly isn't a direct outgrowth of the gospel. On the other hand, something very similar to what has historically been called journaling is found by example in Scripture. King David poured out his soul to God in the scrolls of the Psalms. The prophet Jeremiah expressed to God the depth of his grief about the fall of Jerusalem in his Lamentations. Of course, unlike the words of David and Jeremiah in Scripture, no believer's writings today are divinely inspired. But the examples of these men in writing their prayers, meditations, questions, and so on provide scriptural validation for encouraging contemporary Christians to consider the value of doing the same in a journal.

Value of Journaling

Keeping a journal not only promotes spiritual growth by means of its own virtues, but it's a valuable aid to many other aspects of the spiritual life. Consider what journaling has to offer in these areas:

Help in self-understanding and evaluation. One of the ways the "progress or decline of the inner man" can be noted through journaling is by the observation of previously undetected patterns in your life.[1] When I review my journal entries for a month, six months, or a year, I usually see myself and events more objectively. I can analyze my thoughts and actions apart from the feelings I had at the time. From that perspective it's easier to observe whether I've made spiritual progress or have backslidden in a particular area.

Used appropriately, a journal can actually become a means of propelling us into action for others. The journal can be a mirror in which we see more clearly our attitudes, thoughts, words, and actions. Since we will be held accountable for each of these at the Judgment, evaluating them by *any* means is wisdom.

Help in meditation. I believe meditation on Scripture (compare Joshua 1:8; Psalm 1:1-3) is the single greatest devotional need of most Christians. However, meaningful meditation requires a concentration not often developed in our fast-paced, media-distracted society. Sitting with pen and paper or fingers floating above the keys also heightens my expectation of hearing from God as I think on Him and His words in the passage before me. When I record in a journal my meditations on a passage of Scripture, I simply focus on the text better and find meditation more fruitful.

Help in expressing thoughts and feelings to the Lord. A journal is a place where we can give expression to the fountain of our heart, where we can unreservedly pour out our passion before the Lord. By slowing us down and prompting us to think more deeply about God, journaling helps us feel more deeply (and biblically) about God.

Help in remembering the Lord's works. Many people think God has not blessed them with much until they have to move it all to a new address. In the same way, we tend to forget just how many times God has answered specific prayers, made timely provision, and done marvelous things in our lives. But having a place to collect all these memories prevents their being forgotten.

Help in creating and preserving a spiritual heritage. Journaling is an effective way of teaching the things of God to our children and grandchildren, and of transmitting our faith into the future (compare Deuteronomy 6:4-7; 2 Timothy 1:5). There could be an unimaginable future spiritual impact in something we write today.

Help in clarifying and articulating insights. I've discovered that if I write down the meditations of my quiet time with the Lord, they stay with me much longer. Without journaling, by day's end I often can remember little from my devotional time.

Help in monitoring goals and priorities. A journal is a good way to keep before us the things we want to do and emphasize. Some put a list of goals and priorities in their journal and review it every day.

Help in maintaining the other Spiritual Disciplines. My journal is the place where I record my progress with all the Spiritual Disciplines. Recording the joys and freedom I experience through the Spiritual Disciplines is another way journaling helps maintain my involvement with them. The Christian life is, by definition, a living thing. If we can think of the Discipline of Bible intake as its food and prayer as its breath, many Christians have made journaling its heart. For them it pumps life-maintaining blood into every Discipline connected with it.

Ways of Journaling

How is it done? "Your way of keeping a journal is the right way. . . . There are no rules for keeping a journal!"[2] Many Christians find that the most practical approach is to use everyday notebook paper or common printer paper. While some choose a spiral-bound notebook and others prefer a professionally bound journal, I find loose-leaf pages more workable. Some feel strongly about journaling only by hand, that it's more spontaneous and expressive. I'm a big fan of fountain pens and use one every day, but I find that the speed and other advantages of a digital method normally tip the scale for me to journal by that means more often than not.

As a starting entry for each day, try listing the one verse or idea from your Bible reading that impressed you most. Meditate on that for a few minutes, then record your thoughts and insights. From there consider adding recent events in your life and your feelings and responses to them, brief prayers, joys, successes, failures, quotations, and so on. Consider journaling, not only as a way to raise up a "monument to God's faithfulness" in your life,[3] but more importantly "for the purpose of godliness." (Taken from chapter 11 of *Spiritual Disciplines for the Christian Life.*)

LEARNING . . . FOR THE PURPOSE OF GODLINESS

Why do many Christians live as though they've been told, "Choose you this day whom you will serve: scholarship or devotion"? I maintain that the more Christlike we grow, the more we will pursue both a full head and a full heart, and the more we will radiate both spiritual light and heat. Christians must realize that just as a fire cannot blaze without fuel, so burning hearts are not kindled by brainless heads. We must not content ourselves to be like those the Bible condemns as having "a zeal for God, but not according to knowledge" (Romans 10:2).

Does this mean we must be brilliant to be Christians? Absolutely not. But it does mean that to be like Jesus we must be learners, even as He was at only age twelve, "sitting among the teachers, listening to them and asking them questions" (Luke 2:46). An examination of the New Testament word *disciple* reveals that it means to be not only "a follower" of Christ but also "a learner."

In Proverbs 10:14 we're told, "The wise lay up knowledge." The Hebrew word here means "to store up like a treasure." Wise men and women love to learn because they realize that knowledge is like a precious treasure. A wise person not only "acquires" knowledge, he or she "seeks" it (Proverbs 18:15).

In Proverbs 23:12, we're commanded, "Apply your heart to instruction and your ear to words of knowledge." No matter how much previous instruction you have received, nor how extensive your knowledge—especially about God, Christ, the Bible, and the Christian life—and regardless of how intelligent or slow you consider yourself, you still need to apply your heart and ears to learn, for you haven't learned it all.

Fulfilling the Greatest Commandment

Part of God's greatest commandment, said Jesus, is "Love the Lord your God . . . with all your mind" (Mark 12:29-30). What God wants most from you is your love. And one of the ways He wants you to show love and obedience to Him is by godly learning. God is glorified when we use the mind He made to learn of Him, His ways, His Word, and His world. Unless we love God with a growing mind, we will be Christian versions of the Samaritans to whom Jesus said, "You worship what you do not know" (John 4:22).

Learning—Essential for Increased Godliness

The Christian life begins with learning—learning the gospel. No one is made right with God unless he or she learns about Him and His message to the world, a message of good news called the gospel. No one believes in Jesus or loves Jesus unless he or she has heard the story of Jesus and has at least a minimal understanding of it. And just as we cannot *believe* in and *love* Him about whom we've *learned nothing*, so we cannot *grow* in our faith and love of Him unless we *learn more* about Him.

God's truth must be understood before it can be applied. The Word of God must first go through your head if it's going to change your heart and your life. That's why the apostle Paul said, "Do not be conformed to this world, but be *transformed* by the renewal of your *mind*" (Romans 12:2, emphasis added). Christlike transformation of the heart and life—growth in godliness—involves a mental renewal that cannot happen without learning.

No one grows into Christlikeness without a knowledge of it—what Christlikeness looks like, how to cultivate it, why it's necessary, where it leads, and more. If you know little *about* godliness, you will grow little *in* godliness. To know it requires the Discipline of learning.

Learning Is Mostly by Discipline, not by Accident

We must not assume that we have learned true wisdom just by growing older. The observation found in Job 32:9 is, "The abundant in years may not be wise" (NASB). Age and experience by themselves don't increase your spiritual maturity. Becoming like Jesus doesn't happen incidentally or automatically with the passing of birthdays. Godliness, as 1 Timothy 4:7 says, requires a deliberate discipline. The Discipline of learning transforms accidental learners into *intentional* learners.

Learning in a Variety of Ways

- Listen to recorded books.
- Listen to audio and video recordings via the Internet.
- Listen to Bible teaching programs of reputable ministers.
- Use study guides for books when available.
- Prepare good questions in order to dialogue meaningfully with spiritually mature Christians.
- Read the best books.

Above all, remember that learning has a goal. The goal is Christlikeness. Jesus said in Matthew 11:28-29, "Come to me, all who labor and are heavy laden, and I will give you rest. Take my yoke upon you, and *learn* from *me*" (emphasis added). There is a false or superficial knowledge that "puffs up" (1 Corinthians 8:1), but godly learning leads to godly living. (Taken from chapter 12 of *Spiritual Disciplines for the Christian Life*.)

Value of Journaling

3. Why is it important to record the works and ways of God in your life?

_____

_____

Discuss the benefits of journaling in order to chart your progress in the other Spiritual Disciplines. If you have journaled and are willing to do so, share with the group some of what you discovered.

4. How might journaling aid you in doing what Romans 12:3 tells us to do? In biblical meditation?

_____

_____

_____

_____

5. Read Psalm 77:11-12. Which "deeds of the LORD" should you write down and preserve?

_____

_____

_____

6. What do we learn about creating and preserving a spiritual heritage from these verses?

Deuteronomy 6:4-7 _____

_____

_____

2 Timothy 1:5 _____

_____

_____

7. Why is self-accountability so important in our Christian walk?

_____

_____

_____

8. Why is journaling important even when you don't feel like doing it?

_____

_____

_____

9. What type of journal format would be most suitable for you? Why?

_____

_____

_____

The Value of Learning

10. Have you ever known a professing Christian who deliberately chose not to learn new things? Or a believer who sought learning continually? What did you observe about each?

_____

_____

_____

11. What is your personal view of the importance of seeking wisdom and knowledge? What do the following Proverbs say about this?

9:9 _____

_____

10:14 _____

_____

18:15 _____

_____

23:12 _____

_____

12. How does Mark 12:29-30 help you to better understand the importance of godly learning?

_____

_____

_____

13. In Romans 12:2, what does God call us to do?

_____

_____

_____

_____

Learning Is Mostly by Discipline, not by Accident

14. Do you agree that "those who are not *trying* to learn will only get spiritual and biblical knowledge by accident or convenience" (see page 279 in *Spiritual Disciplines for the Christian Life*)? Explain your answer.

_____

_____

_____

15. What role do you think parents play in teaching their children to become intentional learners?

16. Review the ways in which you can learn intentionally. Which ones might help you this week?

17. Do you agree that "growing Christians are reading Christians" (page 282 in *Spiritual Disciplines for the Christian Life*)? Why or why not?

18. If you are not a consistent reader, could you begin the "one-page-per-day" reading habit?[4] If so, what book would you begin?

19. What is offered in Proverbs 13:4 to intentional, disciplined learners who seek knowledge and wisdom in order to love God more and become more Christlike?

CLOSING PRAYER

Ask God to help you cultivate a desire for learning more about Him and His Word and to realize the importance of journaling in that process. Thank Him for providing His Word, in which we can discover His truths, and for giving us the Holy Spirit to teach us.

GOING DEEPER

(Extra questions for further study)

20. What changes are you willing to make in order to create the opportunity to journal regularly?

21. What do you think of the theory that many do not read as adults because to them "reading" means being required to read poorly written textbooks about subjects that did not interest them?

22. What steps will you take this week to learn more about God and what it means to be godly?

23. If you are a parent, what will you do to help your child(ren) learn intentionally about God and His Word?

24. What price are you willing to pay to become a more disciplined, intentional learner rather than an accidental and by convenience learner?

NOTES

LESSON 1: The Spiritual Disciplines . . . for the Purpose of Godliness
1. I capitalize "Spiritual Disciplines" in these pages to call attention to the term as the subject of the book and to help the reader think of these biblical practices as a group.

LESSON 2: Bible Intake (Part 1) . . . for the Purpose of Godliness
1. Jeremiah Burroughs, *Gospel Worship* (1648; reprint, Ligonier, PA: Soli Deo Gloria Publications, 1990), 200.
2. George Gallup, *100 Questions and Answers: Religion in America* (Princeton Religious Research Center, 1989), cited in *USA Today*, February 1, 1990.
3. *Bookstore Journal*, as quoted in *Discipleship Journal*, issue 52, 10.
4. R. C. Sproul, *Knowing Scripture* (Downers Grove, IL: InterVarsity Press, 1977), 17.

LESSON 3: Bible Intake (Part 2) . . . for the Purpose of Godliness
1. J. I. Packer, foreword to R. C. Sproul, *Knowing Scripture* (Downers Grove, IL: InterVarsity, 1979), 9–10.

LESSON 4: Prayer . . . for the Purpose of Godliness
1. John Piper, *Desiring God: Meditations of a Christian Hedonist* (Portland, OR: Multnomah, 1986), 147.
2. W. Farmer, "Memoir of the Author," in William Bates, *The Whole Works of the Rev. W. Bates*, arr. and rev. W. Farmer (reprint, Harrisburg, PA: Sprinkle, 1990), vol. 1, viii.
3. William Bates, *The Whole Works of the Rev. W. Bates*, arr. and rev. W. Farmer (reprint, Harrisburg, PA: Sprinkle, 1990), vol. 3, 130.
4. Andrew Murray, *With Christ in the School of Prayer* (Old Tappan, NJ: Spire Books, 1975), 33.
5. J. C. Ryle, *A Call to Prayer* (Grand Rapids, MI: Baker Book House, 1979), 35.
6. Thomas Manton, *The Complete Works of Thomas Manton* (reprint, Worthington, PA: Maranatha Publications, n.d.), 272–273.

Lesson 5: Worship . . . for the Purpose of Godliness
1. In this chapter I will address only public and private worship, with emphasis on the latter. For a brief biblical, historical, and practical discussion of the subject of family worship, see Donald S. Whitney, *Family Worship: In the Bible, In History, and In Your Home* (Shepherdsville, KY: The Center for Biblical Spirituality, 2005).
2. John Blanchard, comp., *Gathered Gold: A Treasury of Quotations for Christians* (Welwyn, Hertfordshire, England: Evangelical Press, 1984), 342.
3. John Piper, *Desiring God: Meditations of a Christian Hedonist* (Portland, OR: Multnomah, 1986), 70.
4. Geoffrey Thomas, "Worship in Spirit," *The Banner of Truth*, August–September 1987, 8.

Lesson 6: Evangelism . . . for the Purpose of Godliness
1. See J. I. Packer, *Evangelism and the Sovereignty of God* (Downers Grove, IL: InterVarsity Press, 1979), 37–57.
2. George Barna, as quoted in *Discipleship Journal*, issue 49, 40.

Lesson 7: Serving . . . for the Purpose of Godliness
1. C. H. Spurgeon, "Serving the Lord with Gladness," in *Metropolitan Tabernacle Pulpit* (London: Passmore and Alabaster, 1868; reprint, Pasadena, TX: Pilgrim Publications, 1989), vol. 13, 495–496.

Lesson 8: Stewardship . . . for the Purpose of Godliness
1. Jonathan Edwards, "The Preciousness of Time and the Importance of Redeeming It," in *Sermons and Discourses, 1743–1758*, vol. 25 of *The Works of Jonathan Edwards*, ed. Wilson H. Kimnach (New Haven, CT: Yale University Press, 2006), 243–260. Available at Edwards.yale.edu.
2. In this edition of the book, unlike the first, I have usually refrained from including recent statistical information supportive of general statements. What is published as "recent" data soon loses its freshness. And in most cases, a quick search on the Internet can provide the latest information on the matter at hand.

Lesson 9: Fasting, Silence, and Solitude . . . for the Purpose of Godliness
1. Those whose physical health requires balanced meals at all times can observe a partial fast by eating a balanced meal, but not as much as usual. Others may be able to eat just one simple food, such as bread or rice, so that they get what they need but without much of the pleasure of eating. In all such cases, the goal is to get the minimal nutritional intake necessary to prevent physical problems while, if possible, still experiencing at least some hunger or desire for something else. As we'll see later, the person who is fasting *wants* to sense hunger or the desire for more as this becomes a servant to the spiritual purpose of the fast.

2. Or, for those who cannot engage in a normal fast, the following in the text will explain why it is important that they still sense some non-health-threatening degree of desire for more or tastier food.

LESSON 10: Journaling and Learning . . . for the Purpose of Godliness

1. Josiah H. Pratt, ed., *The Thought of the Evangelical Leaders* (James Nisbet, 1856; reprint, Edinburgh, Scotland: The Banner of Truth Trust, 1978), 305.
2. Ronald Klug, *How to Keep a Spiritual Journal* (Nashville, TN: Thomas Nelson, 1982), 58.
3. Edward Donnelly, ed., "The Diary of Thomas Houston of Knockbracken," *The Banner of Truth*, August–September 1989, 11–12.
4. I developed this idea a bit more in "Read One Page Per Day" in *Simplify Your Spiritual Life: Spiritual Disciplines for the Overwhelmed* (Colorado Springs, CO: NavPress, 2003), 111–112.

ABOUT THE AUTHOR

DON WHITNEY has been professor of biblical spirituality and associate dean at the Southern Baptist Theological Seminary in Louisville, Kentucky, since 2005. Before that, he held a similar position (the first such position in the six Southern Baptist seminaries) at Midwestern Baptist Theological Seminary in Kansas City, Missouri, for ten years. He is the founder and president of The Center for Biblical Spirituality. Don is a frequent speaker in churches, retreats, and conferences in the United States and abroad.

Don grew up in Osceola, Arkansas, where he came to believe in Jesus Christ as Lord and Savior. He was active in sports throughout high school and college and worked in the radio station his dad managed.

After graduating from Arkansas State University, Don planned to finish law school and pursue a career in sportscasting. While at the University of Arkansas School of Law, he sensed God's call to preach the gospel of Jesus Christ. He then enrolled at Southwestern Baptist Theological Seminary in Fort Worth, Texas, graduating with a master of divinity degree in 1979. In 1987, Don completed a doctor of ministry degree at Trinity Evangelical Divinity School in

Deerfield, Illinois. He earned a PhD in theology at the University of the Free State in South Africa in 2013.

Prior to his ministry as a seminary professor, Don was pastor of Glenfield Baptist Church in Glen Ellyn, Illinois (a suburb of Chicago), for almost fifteen years. Altogether, he has served local churches in pastoral ministry for twenty-four years.

He is the author of *Spiritual Disciplines for the Christian Life*, which has a companion study guide. He has also written *How Can I Be Sure I'm a Christian?*, *Spiritual Disciplines Within the Church*, *Ten Questions to Diagnose Your Spiritual Health*, *Simplify Your Spiritual Life*, and *Family Worship*. His hobby is restoring and using old fountain pens.

Don lives with his wife, Caffy, in their home near Louisville. She regularly teaches a class for seminary wives; works from their home as an artist, muralist, and illustrator; and enjoys gardening and beekeeping. The Whitneys are parents of Laurelen Christiana.

Don's website address is www.BiblicalSpirituality.org. You can find him on Twitter via @DonWhitney and on Facebook.

DON'T FORGET THE BOOK!

Updated and Revised 20TH Anniversary Edition

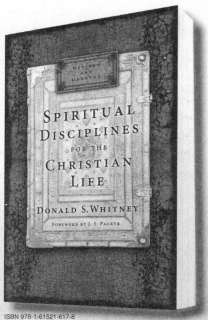

ISBN 978-1-61521-617-8

With new content and a revised cover, this classic teaches
that freedom in Christ leads to discipline in spiritual actions. By practicing and studying ten spiritual disciplines,
you'll discover how Christ's character is then reflected in
your lifestyle. Donald S. Whitney offers practical suggestions for cultivating spiritual disciplines that last long term.

Available wherever books are sold

NAVPRESS